BOOKS BY HERMAN WOUK

NOVELS
Aurora Dawn
City Boy
The Caine Mutiny
Marjorie Morningstar
Youngblood Hawke
Don't Stop the Carnival
The Winds of War
War and Remembrance
Inside, Outside
The Hope
The Glory
A Hole in Texas
The Lawgiver

PLAYS
The Traitor
The Caine Mutiny Court-Martial
Nature's Way

NONFICTON
This Is My God
The Will to Live On
The Language God Talks

HERMAN
WOUK

SAILOR

and

FIDDLER

Reflections

of a

100-Year-Old Author

SIMON & SCHUSTER

New York   London   Toronto   Sydney   New Delhi

Simon & Schuster
1230 Avenue of the Americas
New York, NY 10020

First Simon & Schuster hardcover edition January 2016

SIMON & SCHUSTER and colophon are
registered trademarks of Simon & Schuster, Inc.

For information about special discounts for bulk purchases,
please contact Simon & Schuster Special Sales at
1-866-506-1949 or business@simonandschuster.com.

The Simon & Schuster Speakers Bureau can bring authors to
your live event. For more information or to book an event, contact
the Simon & Schuster Speakers Bureau at 1-866-248-3049
or visit our website at www.simonspeakers.com.

Interior design by Joy O'Meara

Manufactured in the United States of America

1   3   5   7   9   10   8   6   4   2

Library of Congress Cataloging-in-Publication Data
Names: Wouk, Herman, 1915–
Title: Sailor and fiddler : reflections of a 100-year-old author /
Herman Wouk.
Description: New York : Simon & Schuster, 2016.
Identifier: LCCN 2015037994
Subjects: LCSH: Wouk, Herman, 1915– | Authors, American—
20th century—Biography. | BISAC: BIOGRAPHY &
AUTOBIOGRAPHY / Literary. | BIOGRAPHY & AUTOBIOGRAPHY /
Military. | BIOGRAPHY & AUTOBIOGRAPHY / Religious.
Classification: LCC PS3545.O98 Z46 2016 | DDC 813/.54—dc23
LC record available at http://lccn.loc.gov/2015037994

ISBN 978-1-5011-2854-7
ISBN 978-1-5011-2856-1 (ebook)

To the memory of

David "Mickey" Marcus,
Colonel, United States Army,
volunteered and fell
in Israel's War of Independence 1948,
interred in West Point Military Cemetery

Ilan Ramon,
fighter pilot,
Colonel, Israel Defense Forces,
volunteer astronaut,
United States Space Program,
killed in crash of space shuttle *Columbia* 2003

this book of my literary life and work
is humbly dedicated.

Herman Wouk

CONTENTS

SAILOR
and
FIDDLER

AUTHOR'S NOTE

[Written in 2012]

Well they gave him his orders in Munroe, Virginia

Saying "Steve, you're way behind time

It's not 38, this is Old 97

You must bring her to Spencer on time."

. . .

He was goin' down the grade doing 90 miles an hour

When the whistle broke into a scream

He was found in the wreck with his hand on the throttle

He was scalded to death by the steam . . .

—"THE WRECK OF OLD 97"

GENTLE READER, THAT RAILROAD folk tune is sure haunting your durable storyteller, aged ninety-seven.

When I passed my ninetieth milestone going hell-for-leather down the nonagenarian grade, I figured I had better cobble up what was left to write while

I could. A short book called *A Child's Garden of God* waited its turn, a simple essay on faith and science, so I thought, and I took it on. Next thing I knew four years had whistled by, I had in hand two bank boxes crammed with thirty-odd work journals, and a slim book of 40,000 words, *The Language God Talks*. That is a phrase Richard Feynman tossed off when we first met, urging me to learn calculus (which I never did). Years later at the Aspen Institute in Colorado, he and I got into science and faith and much besides, in long rambles on the hiking paths. I thought of calling the book *God and Dick Feynman*, for it does turn on those colloquies; but the great physicist was talking with me, after all, not God, so I dropped that notion.

Well, next on my agenda down the steepening grade was *The Lawgiver*, a novel about Moses, just a few notes filed away for half a century; the "impossible novel," I called it, because it seemed so far beyond my powers. At the moment, hot off the press, *The Lawgiver* lies on my desk, for ignoring the odds, I took heart and wrote it anyway. Good fortune attend it! I ventured out on the old game just for the love of it. Now there's *Sailor and Fiddler* to write, offering my view of this strange life from the vantage of ninety-seven years.

On Old 97 the air brakes failed unhappy Steve, hence the wreck. Lord grant that my air brakes hold while I get done all I can, roll into Spencer on time, and hand in my orders.

PART ONE

_____

THE SAILOR

CHAPTER ONE

No Autobiography, and Why Not

YEARS AND YEARS AGO the late British philosopher Isaiah Berlin floored me by saying, "You should write your autobiography."—"Why me? I'm nobody."—"No, no, you've traveled, you've known many people, you have interesting ideas, it would do a lot of good."

I was meeting him at the Athenaeum Club in London on my way home from Auschwitz, where scenes of the *War and Remembrance* miniseries were being filmed. The poisoned cloud of the Chernobyl nuclear explosion still drifted over Eastern Europe, but the gargantuan American TV project, minus some faint-hearted cast members, was soldiering on. I had started

a new novel about Israel's wars, and Sir Isaiah Berlin was a stalwart Zionist, hence my stopover in London. Our friendship had begun years earlier, when he came to our Georgetown home for a seder. He was delivering the Mellon lectures at the National Gallery of Art during the Passover, and I made bold to invite him to our holiday table. Breaking matzoh with a man is not a bad way to get to know him. We stayed in touch after that, and at this meeting he offered an astute précis, as a British Jew and a world-class thinker, of Israel's achievements and perils. He walked out of the Athenaeum with me, and there on Pall Mall he gave me his blessing on the book, and a parting grandfatherly kiss.

On the homeward flight I got to musing about the autobiography. Why not, after all? Biographies of writers were then much in fashion, confessional books by or about Jewish authors all shook up with angst. I was not one of those, and might that not be a piquant novelty? Soon after coming home I mentioned Sir Isaiah's idea to my wife, also my agent. She was on me like a cougar. "Dear," she responded with a cold clear eye for a writer's dodge, "you're not that interesting a person. What is it that you don't want to write?" I had read her my start on the Israel novel, and she had said, "You've got me interested," so I had pushed on, trying to bring

to life an invented TV journalist assigned to cover Israel, so as to put American eyes into the story. The last I remember, this journalist was standing on his head in a room full of books, I no longer know why. My wife wanted to know more about the upside-down fellow, but I did not, he was a lifeless puppet. Now I told her as much. "Well, then," says she with great good cheer, "pull up your socks and start over." So I did. End of autobiography brain wave.

Through several years spent partly in Israel, I wrote *The Hope* and *The Glory*; and I stand by the military history in the books, accurate as I could make it about wars still much in controversy. The personal story intertwines the lives and loves of some army families over two generations, with no American journalist as camera eye. "Oh, you're not making it an *army* story, are you?" cries a wise old Israeli on reading a few early draft chapters. "There's so much more to Israel than the army!" True, but I am not an Israeli, and those depths were not available for me. Somerset Maugham said that his novels were largely his autobiography, and in my way I have used up my own life, pretty near, in my fiction. That is what the Sailor part of this book is about. Those Israeli novels actually shade over into the Fiddler aspect of the book, which we will get to in due course.

The Sea Beast

A bright red hardcover book, *The Sea Beast,* got me going in Literature.

The year was 1927, which for some readers may merge with 1776. It was the year "Lucky" Lindbergh flew over the ocean nonstop to Paris. I was twelve. The book was the novelized screenplay of a silent movie about a ship's captain whose leg got half bitten off by a whale. The scene that caused all the buzz, and the lines at the movie theaters, showed the captain agonizing in clouds of steam as the raw bloody stump was cauterized. The novelized screenplay was very long, the print was very small, and the end hard to figure out. Had the captain really killed the whale, or not? In the movie, no problem; he not only killed it dead, he then stumped back to Nantucket, rescued his sweetheart from his evil brother, and lived happily ever after. But the book said only, about the harpooning, "The stricken whale flew forward." To me that word "stricken" meant the whale was done for. My softhearted sister ruled no, not necessarily, maybe the poor sea beast got away with the harpoon stuck in it. She had bought the book, she was fifteen. That was that.

A preface to the screenplay insisted the changes in the movie were not "presumptuous meddling," which puzzled me. Movies *always* changed the books. Tom Sawyer in the movie, for instance, had been a big plump clumsy kid, hardly more Mark Twain's Tom than he was a white whale. In the novelized screenplay, there was no cauterizing scene at all, and this Captain Ahab had no brother and no sweetheart, either. Strange business! About that time, I found in the public library a fat book, *Moby-Dick; or, The Whale,* and flipped through it. *Lo and behold,* The Sea Beast *screenplay, word for word!* That explained the small print, and such was my introduction to "presumptuous meddling." The theme may recur in this non-autobiography. The silent-film freebooters just helped themselves to this overblown old sea yarn and did what they pleased with it, just as they did with *Anna Karenina,* in which Greta Garbo didn't die, not on your life.

Herman Melville; or, Literature

Once, while writing *The Language God Talks,* I went to Princeton to consult a savant who had known Feyn-

man well, and I got shanghaied into giving an annual lecture on physics. The scheduled eminent physicist didn't show, and to be a good fellow when asked, I waffled my way through twenty minutes, mostly by joshing about my ignorance of the subject. Afterward, someone in the crowded lecture hall (a Nobel physicist, I later learned) stood up and asked whether there existed in novel writing anything like the "aha" moment in science. "Absolutely," I said, "it comes thirty years after you're dead." As an ex-gagman's snappy comeback, it got a laugh. As a one-line response to the query, it was the strange and bitter truth about Herman Melville's life and work.

Literature, I tell aspiring writers, is a mug's game. The author of *Moby-Dick* died in his seventies utterly forgotten, everything he wrote long out of print. Not one newspaper obituary noted his passing. Some thirty years after he died—about the time *The Sea Beast* was cleaning up at the box office—the academic field of American literature was swamped by a tsunami of second thoughts about Melville. A Columbia professor of my time, Raymond Weaver, led it off with a respectful biography, discovering the unpublished manuscript of *Billy Budd* during his research. Professor Weaver has since been lost in the crush, but he beat them all to Herman Melville's "aha" moment,

no contest. Today in the University of Chicago's *Great Books of the Western World, Moby-Dick* is volume 48 out of 54, and Melville is right up there with Aristotle, Shakespeare, Cervantes, Tolstoy, and Marx; no Balzac volume, by the by, no Dickens, no Henry James, no Twain, no Proust, no Joyce. A mug's game, I say, a crapshoot, the stakes one's heart's blood. Young aspirers to Literature who face the stakes open-eyed, yet roll the dice, have my grandfatherly blessing and a ghostly kiss.

Writing for a living is something else entirely. The distinction should clear up as we go along here.

Twain

A door-to-door book salesman sold my mother a set of green-bound books by "the American Shalom Aleichem," and so Mark Twain came into my ken. I was a cormorant reader, voraciously downing hardcovers traded by us urchins on the street—*Baseball Joe, Tarzan, Rover Boys, Tom Swift*—and lots of public library books. The hardcovers were peanuts to be shelled and eaten, the library books were passable nourishment. Twain was a bombshell, a beam of blaz-

ing morning sun in our fifth-floor back flat. His books were life itself, warm laughing life. Tom and Huck dissolved in my bloodstream. In the longer books—*Innocents Abroad, Roughing It, A Connecticut Yankee,* and the rest—a page or two might be hard going, a passage sad, but the note of wry laughter was continuous under all. Without giving it any thought I was finding my calling; I would be a writer, what was more a *funny* writer, nothing else. Such was the influence of Sam Clemens of Hannibal, Missouri, on a son of Russian-Jewish immigrants in the Bronx, born five years after he died.

Meantime, in Class 8B3 of P.S. 75, Miss Sarah Dickson was introducing us to Literature. Miss Dickson wore her abundant gray hair braided around her head in a net, and she did her Literature thing with zest. She taught us "Evangeline" and "The Courtship of Miles Standish," long Longfellow poems that didn't rhyme like proper poems—say, like "The Raven"—but were composed in dactyls, which made them poetry. To convince us of this, she recited some of the dactyls with combative emphasis: " 'THIS is the FOR est pri ME val,' " and so on. Her abiding challenge was to make eighth-graders appreciate Literature, but such stuff was a tough sell. "Evangeline" and "Miles Standish" were stories, at least, if rather boring and

gummed up by dactyls, but her favorite piece, "Than-atopsis" by one William Cullen Bryant, was a total baffler. It didn't rhyme, it wasn't even in dactyls, and it drove to the unconvincing point that dying was not so bad. Recently on the Internet I chanced upon an exchange between ninth-graders about *The Scarlet Letter,* with comments that would have puzzled Miss Dickson, like "Sucks." Possibly in a time of video games and reality shows, Literature is not for every-body; though, in fact, way back before even radio ex-isted, let alone TV and video games, Miss Dickson did not do much better—at least for me, and I was her pet—at inoculating eighth-graders with Literature.

Dumas

Buried somewhere in a Palm Springs warehouse is the autograph album of my P.S. 75 graduation class. Amid the scrawls of my classmates there is a page of que-ries such as "What do you want to be?" and "Who is your favorite author?" To those I answered, of course, "Writer" and "Mark Twain." Yet, startlingly, Mark Twain is crossed out, and above it is scrawled "Alexan-dre Dumas." DUMAS? Yes, Dumas. Uncle Louie, our

family intellectual, was a pigeon for the book peddlers; they sold him not only Twain but Dickens, O. Henry, Dumas, Maupassant, and more. During family visits, I would poke into those sets. A big blue Dickens book I sampled began with great carrying-on about fog, and no story. I tried *The Black Tulip,* a red-bound Dumas. At the outset a roaring mob lynched two Dutchmen named DeWitt, tore them to bloody pieces, and sold the pieces around town to eat, and then an evil jailer crushed under his heel the bulb of a black tulip worth millions. This guy was pretty good. I sampled and then borrowed from the public library *The Three Musketeers,* after that *The Count of Monte Cristo,* and so on all along the Dumas shelves. Like Twain's laughter in my blood, Dumas narrative lodged in my brain— to remain dormant, however, for decades, since I was going to be a funnyman and nothing else.

Papa

Speaking of influence and of funnymen: my father, the stern busy boss of a steam laundry all week, at dinner Friday night was Papa, convulsing us kids with his drolleries in Yiddish, and his Shalom Aleichem

readings. For folk humor Shalom Aleichem (Sholom Rabinowitz) was Twain's peer, quite as the book peddler told Mama. Yiddish was not a language I had to learn; rather an ambiance absorbed in infancy. Reading Shalom Aleichem today, I hear in his warm clear prose my father's Friday-night voice—the lover of Jewish characters and traditions, the Zionist, the unshakable optimist, the naive American patriot who freed himself from czarist Russia. "If you ever get called into the army," Papa once said, "I'll come and wash the floor of your barracks."

For some of the last century's literary elite, mostly Jewish, my books were outside their "canon" of protest and alienation. They were entitled. They never heard my father read Shalom Aleichem on Friday night.

Big Man on Campus

Inside, Outside, my novel that I call a kaddish for my father, has some painfully funny chapters about my high school years in a downtown public school, Townsend Harris Hall, attended mainly by Manhattan smoothies. Among them I was a Bronx nobody, a fat short baby-faced classroom clown. Depicted in

fiction fifty years later, my teenage ordeals and disasters may be amusing, but I am not revisiting them now, thank you, not for love or money. On to Columbia College, where I found my feet as a funnyman. At the opening night of the 1932 Columbia Varsity Show, as a freshman just starting to shave, I watched awestruck the show's author, a Big Man on Campus, who also wrote comic verse and prose in *Jester* and the "Off-hour" humor column in *Spectator,* singing and dancing before my eyes as Hamlet in his hodgepodge Shakespeare musical.

This was Arnold Auerbach, a Manhattan smoothie and funnyman, who became my Columbia mentor. I joined his Jewish fraternity, I followed him as "Off-hour" columnist, as *Jester* humorist, as Varsity Show author, as Big Man on Campus. I shared his dreams of writing for Broadway. On graduating, since he became a radio gagman, so did I. Full disclosure: in my novel written decades afterward, Arnold morphs into a totally different imaginary figure, the famed novelist Peter Quat; a gifted sex-ridden critics' darling who gives his books titles like *Onan's Way* and *My Cock,* boffs his publisher's wife, and supports several children by several wives. Arnold was genially tolerant of this foolery, having made his name in Broadway musicals, and old Peter Quat remains a favorite creation of mine.

The Gag Czar

Our first employer, David Freedman, lived in a quadru-
plex tower penthouse on Central Park West. When
I came for my job interview, Arnold already worked
there. The Gag Czar was breakfasting on fried matzoh
and pork sausages in midafternoon, paunchy, deathly
pale, looking fresh out of bed. "This is the most ter-
rific dish in America," he greeted me, and with that
declaration he enters *Inside, Outside* as Harry Goldhandler, who keeps up a killing pace of day-and-night
work on three or four weekly radio programs for different comedians. Freedman was a Jewish Phi Bete born
on the Lower East Side, son of a Yiddish newspaper
columnist called Solly the Atheist, and his true forte
was rich Rabelaisian improvising, more than commercial joke-writing. He loved to hold forth with raunchy
Jewish persiflage; publishers, journalists, Broadway
celebrities would come to the penthouse after dinner
just to hear him, cigar in hand, being the Gag Czar.

However, "Goldhandler's" lavish lifestyle in that
penthouse, splendidly furnished on credit—black
gourmet cook, kitchen maid, two housemaids, three
teenage sons, and his wife's live-in parents—depended
on a stream of Madison Avenue money from those

— 15 —

radio scripts; nothing else, for he had nothing else in the world. The cascade abruptly dried up when Freedman's main source, the frenetic song-and-dance man Eddie Cantor, hired away a veteran writer of vaudeville acts who worked on Freedman's staff. The Gag Czar was dropped cold. Cantor's bestselling humorous autobiography, *My Life Is in Your Hands,* ghostwritten by Freedman, had made Cantor popular; and subsequent Freedman funny books, all published as Cantor's work, had sealed his fame.

Show business.

When I was hired, Freedman's decline had just started. Arnold and I soon abandoned him in his fall when we heard that Fred Allen, the one radio funnyman we admired, was losing his chief writer to Hollywood. We applied to Allen as a team and, in due course, got the job. A couple of years after that, "Harry Goldhandler," still in that tower penthouse, worn out by desperate clutching for income here and there, died one night in his sleep. Arnold and I loved the Gag Czar, but youth is cruel and selfish. Besides, it was show business—that is, writing for a living.

Fred Allen: Treadmill to Oblivion

Last night I was roaring with laughter over the yellowed pages of *Treadmill to Oblivion,* Fred Allen's mordant 1954 memoir of his years in radio. John Steinbeck, in a blurb on the faded jacket, calls Fred Allen an American humorist in the manner of Petroleum Nasby and Mark Twain. James Thurber pays him homage as a peer in comic writing. William Faulkner and President Roosevelt were among his multitudinous fans.

Who was this man who baffled and battled the broadcasting pooh-bahs for eighteen years, this great almost forgotten American? A Boston Irishman, to begin with, a high school graduate (he got no further), John Florence Sullivan, who, on taking to the vaudeville stage in his teens, billed himself "Freddy James, the World's Worst Juggler." He rose to appearing as Fred Allen in Broadway musicals of the 1920s. When advertising agencies discovered the new selling gimmick of radio, and further discovered that funnymen drew audiences, he was hired—not for his jokes, as he himself tells it in *Treadmill,* but for his flat nasal voice. His success in radio took time, while more popular comedians were snatching at the easy money that had ensnared the Gag Czar. Nevertheless, Fred Allen's

Town Hall Tonight and *Allen's Alley* did climb to number one and stayed at or near it for years and years, utterly confounding Madison Avenue's highest seers who knew his stuff was "too cerebral." At last one of them was inspired to pit brainless triviality against brilliant wit and intelligent comment. A game show, *Stop the Music,* showed up on another network opposite Fred Allen and caught on. Fred's ratings fell and fell. He was never the same. He persisted for a few more years, but his heart was no longer in the weekly battle with dullards and censors, and bad health made him quit. So passed from the scene this original American humorist, who poured his rare comic powers into two decades of forgotten ephemera.

Treadmill to oblivion, indeed.

But when he took us on he was riding high, and what a contrast to the Gag Czar! The national number one funnyman lived in a two-room suite of an old midtown hotel with his wife and longtime foil, Portland Hoffa. His working habits were the essence of New England parsimony. He wrote the weekly show himself, using our rough drafts to get started. He never praised or blamed us; sometimes he adapted and put in our stuff, sometimes not. He handprinted the script on a single white sheet of nine-by-fourteen paper. When he had filled both sides of the sheet that was

it, an hour-long comedy show, ready to be typed up by a sister-in-law for mimeograph. The rest was rehearsing, revising, performing; then a midnight script confab with "the boys"—Arnold and me—at Joe's, a local eatery, and back to work in the morning on the next program. So it went for five years, which on looking back, I see as a long dream in a featherbed.

An earnest review of *The Lawgiver* crossed my desk this morning, highlighting my Fred Allen years and suggesting that my literary style owes a debt to that experience. Not an unpleasing thought; Twain's high art was rooted in his lecturing career, with its one paramount rule, *hold the audience.* In radio that rule was life or death. If there is a trace of Fred Allen's art in my books, that is all to the good.

The Featherbed

Our five years with Allen slipped by, especially during the thirteen-week summer layoffs, in the pursuit of la dolce vita by young wise guys with money to spend: travel abroad, callow amours, what you will. Now and then we made desultory gestures at collaborating on Broadway farces and musicals, and I expressed an oc-

casional yearning to try Literature. Arnold dismissed this as self-soothing posturing, which no doubt it was. Hitler was on the ascent and black clouds were starting to obscure our sunny Franklin Roosevelt skies. Der Führer smashed into Poland. England and France declared war, and after a winter pause dubbed "the phony war," France fell in three weeks, and bombs rained on London. We chattered quite a bit about all this, and remained as oblivious—so now it seems to me—as well-fed apes in the zoo. Congress passed a draft bill. Draft boards formed all over the country, but not in or near Radio City. German armies marched into the Soviet Union, Roosevelt and Churchill met in Newfoundland, and the draft was renewed by *one* vote. Arnold and I duly received draft notices. The show went on getting laughs and we got our paychecks. Our girls were pretty, Dinty Moore's steaks were great, and we had great seats for all the new Broadway hits.

Once on a Plan B impulse, I inquired at a Navy recruiting office about volunteering for reserve officer training. The Navy wanted, I learned, only applicants with engineering degrees. I asked the ensign on duty what I might do about this. "Go to engineering school," he airily suggested, and I skulked out.

_____

On the morning of December 8, 1941, the day after the day that would live in infamy, my brother-in-law phoned me at seven A.M. I had been working all night, rewriting a radio script instantly outdated by Pearl Harbor. "Do you have this week's *New Yorker?*"—Me, blearily, "Sure, why?"—"Take a look at the bottom of page ninety-seven. The small Navy ad." I did. I got up, showered, dressed, and caught a cab. The Navy was being forehanded enough, as the President's negotiations with the Japanese dragged on, to start trolling for reserve officer recruits, age eighteen to twenty-seven (I was now over twenty-six), two years minimum of college, nothing about engineering school. The place to apply was a Navy training vessel tied up at a wharf on the East River. Sober-faced collegians were waiting there in the wardroom for interviews, and more were arriving as I signed in, a decidedly old fellow among them. They were summoned into another room one by one while I collected my thoughts. The gag-writing team had broken up in the summer break, Arnold had married and gone off to Hollywood, and I was writing a program promoting defense bonds for the U.S. Treasury, a summer replacement for the Allen show. When Fred

returned in the fall, *The Treasury Hour* had moved to another network, and I had gone with it, writing for a living.

That was where I stood in life when my name was called.

The Green Table

Behind a table covered with green baize, five blue and gold uniforms confronted me. Questions came at me from five faces more or less alike. Why was I applying for midshipman school at my age? What was my major in college? What was my favorite sport? My physical condition? The grayhead in the center was looking through a folder on the desk. He spoke up.

"Have you received a draft notice?"

"Yes, sir, I have."

"And an army medical?"

"Yes." Knees shaking.

"Then you're ineligible, sir." Chill note of authority. "You must know that."

"No, sir," I managed to articulate. "I was not aware of that." Long pause. Grayhead closed the folder and tapped it. "I see you've written for Fred Allen."

"Yes, sir. For five years, until last June."

The faces changed. All were regarding me with lively interest. The senior officer: "What's Fred Allen like? Is he funny in real life?"

My knees firmed: familiar ground. The younger officers spoke up with more questions about Fred Allen, clearly a spell of relief from the interviewing chore. The grayhead put an end to it. "Well, sir, the Navy could have used you, but you have your draft notice and the Army has got first call on you." He shrugged and half smiled. "Maybe a man who writes for Fred Allen can do something about that."

The nearest telephone booth was in a drugstore. I called Fred and told him of the interview. "I see." Old familiar twang. "Come up here." I found him typing as usual at the desk piled with newspaper clippings, books, and papers. He glanced through the papers and handed one to me. "Take a look at this. Is it all right?" It was a flawlessly typed letter to my draft board—all lowercase, no capitals—on one letterhead sheet with the famous Fred Allen caricature by Hirschfeld: shirtsleeves, eyeshade, overflowing desk, baggy eyes, worried face. He was recommending me as a naval officer, in a deadpan vein that nevertheless made me laugh out loud. "How's Arnold? I hear he's settled down in Hollywood, waiting for nibbles." Fred

waved off my thanks, turned back to his typewriter, and was clicking away as I left.

My draft board office was uptown on the West Side, a nondescript storefront lined with steel files, a nondescript man at a battered desk. Nobody else was there. He took Allen's letter from me with a bored air, glancing from the letter back to me, and began to laugh and laugh. "Fred Allen, eh? What's he like? Is he funny in real life?" I gave him a hearty honest answer. "Five years, eh? And now you're applying for Naval Reserve training?" With that, so help me, he swivels around and types out on a government form my release from the army draft.

"What's in a name?" says lovesick Juliet. "That which we call a rose by any other name would smell as sweet . . ."

Back at the green table, where the five officers still sat, by now looking weary, I handed the draft release to the senior officer. He raised his eyebrows over it. "Well done," he allowed himself to say.

Truth to tell, I don't much recall the rest. Remember, all this happened seventy-two years ago. I was *in*. That I can tell you. In the United States Naval Reserve, thanks to the name of Fred Allen, with one foot firmly planted on a treadmill to Literature.

CHAPTER TWO

Not That Interesting a Person

Aurora Dawn

THAT AN INSIGNIFICANT GAGMAN like me could ever write a book at all, let alone a novel, was not in my plans or my dreams. My vague immediate plan, as I went to sea, was to write Broadway plays and bring back a sheaf when peace came. I did write one aboard the *John B. Floyd,* the Liberty ship in which I sailed to the South Pacific; twenty-seven days without sighting land, all kinds of time. On the U.S.S. *Zane* (DMS 14), the old destroyer-minesweeper to which I reported, I wrote a second play, a third, started a fourth and halted. This was not like writing Fred Allen skits after

all. If I had an aptitude for Broadway entertainment, it was not surfacing.

What, then? I had laughed out loud just thinking about the plot and the title for the fourth play, *Aurora Dawn*. *Aurora Dawn* was a soap. The plot concerned a radio preacher who soared to such astronomic ratings that he could tangle head-on with the bullying know-nothing soap magnate and his craven admen, and prevail. I don't know why I decided to start over and write this gagman fantasy as a novel. To this day I truly don't. I had no such serious aspirations. On graduating from college I had written a couple of *New Yorker* stories that hadn't sold, and that had been that. The jokes for the Gag Czar had paid well. The Fred Allen jokes had earned me Saks Fifth Avenue clothes, a roof away from my parents' home, and bread: that is to say, eating on Fred's tab at Joe's, and where I pleased in New York's fine restaurants.

Elsewhere I have written that this turn to fiction came from my reading *Don Quixote* at the time.* Well, could be. It could also be that for once I was not writing for a living; after all, the Navy was feeding, clothing, and sheltering me. I remember starting *Au-*

---

* *The Language God Talks*, Little, Brown and Company, New York and Boston, 2010.

rora Dawn, the novel, as sheer fun, taking the mock-heroic voice of Henry Fielding and capering around in it with sophomoric exuberance. The first page was scrawled on the *Zane* in 1943 off Guadalcanal, and *Aurora Dawn* is still in print, so if my cheeky first pass at fiction would interest the reader now, it is there on Kindle and in paperback. When it came out after the war, it encountered predictable assaults, a little nice praise, and a book club co-selection. *The New Yorker* disapproved in a red rage.

You may well ask, how could a raw ensign on a warship find time to write at all? Well, there were warships, and then again there was the *Zane.* My writing lapsed after two chapters, when a new captain took over the *Zane,* and I turned my attention to surviving. Not until after the war did I finish *Aurora Dawn* and start my next book, in a small rented house on Long Island, where a very lively baby showed up in my life, nine months after I got out of the Navy and into matrimony. My publisher, charmed by my pseudo-Fielding prose, offered me a job in public relations as a sideline, at a tempting salary. I thought, Well, with my new responsibilities, why not? My wife told me why not, in a scary outburst that blew away the newlywed love haze and began to define her. "WHAT? How *dare* he, how DARE he interfere with your *writing*? NO!"

I listened. Working ahead on the new novel, a pastiche of *Tom Sawyer* as *Aurora Dawn* was of *Tom Jones,* I bore strongly in mind a lesson learned in Navy gunnery drills: first shot over the target, okay; second shot short of the target, less okay, third shot had better be right on. Though urban boyhood novels were then all squalid and violent, *Herbie, the City Boy* was coming out idyllic and funny, a defiant minor try, well short of the target. For that all-important next shot, I had two notions—a send-up of my sister and her boyfriends, or maybe a comic picture of a nutty ship's captain. I started two new work journals, *Marjorie's Lovers* and *The Year of Captain Horrocks.* "Horrocks" was just a creepy name for the captain. Marjorie was my actual college love, dubbed by many foiled swains the Iceberg; among them she froze me, and showed up decades later as Dorsi Sabin in *Inside, Outside.* (Revenge, revenge!) "Marjorie" became the heroine's name in the book about my sister. Captain Horrocks became Captain Queeg.

Over the decades many many people in various walks of life, military and civilian, have told me that they once had a Captain Queeg. He has passed into literature, yet his strange doings on the *Zane* were almost not written down at all, and nobody the wiser. As I write (May 2013), the unveiling of my wife's

headstone is a few weeks away. Here is a reminiscence of her, filling out those few words (mostly Hebrew) cut in cold granite. Betty Sarah Wouk, the beautiful love of my life, probably saved the *Zane* saga from evanescing unrecorded when a distinguished German-Jewish composer came close to derailing my life as a budding novelist.

Kurt Weill

Forced to flee by the Nazis, Kurt Weill had made a second successful career in the United States, composing Broadway musicals and movie scores. I met him through a Broadway wannabe I hardly knew, long on connections but short on talent, who phoned me to say Kurt Weill wanted to meet me. We three met and this go-between took instant charge, declaring that the notion of an *Aurora Dawn* musical was inspired, he would direct it, and write the libretto with me. Weill, a short quiet man, said little but that he liked my book. I said I might write the libretto, but collaborate, no, no way. At this, the wannabe exploded in a mushroom-cloud huff, and the meeting adjourned.

Later I heard from Weill himself, and we hit it

off. Kurt Weill had a Fred Allen–like authority about musical shows, a soft-spoken Jew, wearing lightly his renown for "Mack the Knife" and "September Song." In our confabs an exciting vision of a musical show quickly took form, and he suggested that we meet for dinner with our wives. So the European chanteuse Lotte Lenya and my California ex–Navy Department gal got acquainted in a kosher Manhattan restaurant. We all laughed a lot, the wives clearly enjoyed each other, Kurt reminisced about his boyhood as a cantor's son, and I had my Navy and gagman stories.

Driving back to Long Island amid wind and rain, in a glow of stimulated good feeling, I remarked that the musical looked set, and I would love doing it. "I think you should write that crazy captain book first," she responded. "That one sounds good." I was brought up short. The new postwar novelists had been racing past and trampling me, Tom Heggen with *Mr. Roberts,* Ross Lockridge with *Raintree County,* and as for Arnold Auerbach, he had galloped way ahead and out of sight with *Call Me Mister,* an Army musical revue, the hottest ticket on Broadway. Weill's *Aurora Dawn* seemed by far my best shot to get back in the game.

Brought up short—yet a voice in my soul said, over the slap-slap of the windshield wipers, "Listen to her." I can put it no other way. I didn't hear her loud and

clear, her words were slow and thoughtful, as though half to herself. Next day I phoned Kurt. My new book was almost done, I told him, I had another book to write that might take a year, and if he could wait, I would do the musical with delight. Not put out at all, he promised to stay in touch, and true to his word, he called me at intervals while he wrote two new shows. I was half through drafting *The Caine Mutiny* when his latest musical opened in triumph. He phoned, elated by his success, and we agreed to meet and clear our lives to do *Aurora Dawn* next. Not long after that, I opened *The New York Times* one morning to learn that Kurt Weill had suddenly died at fifty.

That Crazy Captain Book

How long ago all this was!

Had I gone along with the bonhomie of that kosher dinner and embarked on the Weill musical, who can say? The long, lonely stony uphill way of the novel was (and remains) a daunting alternative to the fleshpots of showbiz. Churchill wrote of war making, "The terrible ifs accumulate." It is just as true of art. I will always believe that if not for my wife's word in sea-

son, the story of Captain Queeg might well have remained untold. As things turned out, few stories of
World War II are better known. The movie, the novel,
and the play are part of general culture. I did write
The Caine Mutiny in a year, which I can now scarcely
believe. As John Steinbeck said of his quickly written
early work, "I was hungry then." I read the book to my
wife chapter by chapter as I wrote it. At one point she
remarked, "If they don't like this one, you had better
try another line of business."

It looked for a while like I might have to do just
that. The prestigious publisher who first read the
manuscript rejected it outright ("Obviously the story
should start on the ship. The author's reach exceeds
his grasp"). A commercial house did venture a substantial advance for my Navy book (plus, however, a
second book to follow it). Bemused by this windfall
of big bucks, we unwisely bought a mansion in Great
Neck. After that, book clubs, magazines, movie book
buyers, all were totally uninterested; then, a giant bestseller about the Army, *From Here to Eternity,* came
out a few weeks before *The Caine Mutiny,* sweeping
the country's critics and swamping the bookstores.
Captain Queeg was born in total eclipse. This fateful
mischance, with the arrival in the mansion of a second baby son, unnerved us; we put the mansion on

the market and moved to Mexico to reduce expenses. There, in a rented house in Cuernavaca, we lost our firstborn son, Abe. The "very lively baby," grown to a sagacious little boy almost five, lovable and winsome beyond telling, drowned in the swimming pool. I have not written, nor will I, about this catastrophe, from which we never wholly recovered.

———

"Fiddler" in my book's title refers of course to the Broadway Jewish musical *Fiddler on the Roof,* which made of Shalom Aleichem's dairyman Tevye a beloved world legend of humble faith. A skilled writer of biographies* once offered to quarry my life story out of the daily journals I have kept since 1937. She read several volumes and reluctantly concluded that two strands ran through them: the literary life, which she would have handled with pleasure; and my "spiritual journey," which only I could write. That is the Fiddler thread of all my work: muted here, but darkening and deepening ever since Cuernavaca. To the Sailor thread I now return.

---

* Meryle Secrest: Leonard Bernstein, Stephen Sondheim, Salvador Dalí, Bernard Berenson, etc.

———

With moral strength that welded us for life, my wife bore up on our return from Mexico with Abe's body and the baby Nathaniel. She managed the funeral, the mourning, and the condolence visits of family and friends, while I was sunk in grief-stricken collapse. I began to come out of it in the bar of the Carlyle Hotel in Manhattan. It is my first clear recollection of that time. What I was doing at the Carlyle, I have no idea. I noticed on another table a copy of *The Caine Mutiny*, the first I had seen since Mexico. I was dimly aware that the book had begun climbing the bestseller lists; beyond that, blackness. I went to that table, showed the couple sitting there my picture on the back of the garish jacket, and inscribed the book for them, to their pleased stupefaction. In a month or so my novel overtook *From Here to Eternity*, became an astounding literary surprise, and led the bestseller lists for the better part of two years.

Marjorie

———

Work is the anodyne of anodynes. Settled in a small rental apartment in mid-Manhattan, I went back to

work. The first words of *Marjorie's Lovers* compared a seventeen-year-old girl to a naval mine drifted up on a beach: ominous, intimidating, sooner or later bound to explode. The novel now starts with her mother looking in at her asleep, the morning after a college dance. Same idea, less extravagantly put. Marjorie wakes, turns on the hot water in the shower, and in the clouds of billowing vapor has a revelation: she is going to become an actress! My own mother's maternal family name was Morgenstern—Yiddish for Morningstar—and I had made it the girl's family name. In a flash she fuses it with Marjorie for a spine-tingling stage name she can *see* in electric lights; and the novel for all time becomes *Marjorie Morningstar.*

Writing it was slow going at first. The publisher was printing 50,000 copies of *The Caine Mutiny* at a crack. Such a huge success can paralyze an author, but that was not it at all. I had three novels under my belt, and the second, *City Boy,* had been thrown out by the publisher to die: little promotion, less advertising, the title changed without a by-your-leave, Wouk a discarded flash in the pan. All that was behind me. *Marjorie* was a profound challenge I did not yet fathom, that was my trouble. You meet her through the eyes of her parents, you see her last in middle age as an old admirer glimpses her, and in between, for more than

five hundred pages, you as reader are trapped inside a growing girl's head. A bizarre unplanned structure! I groped to it, and that is more or less how I have written my novels. The theme has been there for a while, sometimes for a long while. Its time comes. The characters show up, often from my own life, and start acting it out.

———

Around then, for instance, I read in *Life* magazine an article about Admiral William F. "Bull" Halsey and the Battle of Leyte Gulf. Called "The Battle of Bull's Run," it sketched in a couple of pages the greatest sea battle in history. The *Zane* had towed gunnery drill targets for Halsey's fleet as it sortied from Ulithi atoll for Leyte, and as communications officer, I had read all the fragmentary, excited, strident, utterly confusing dispatch traffic of the battle. Like my fellow officers, I was coping with the tantrums and edicts of the captain, and the giant far-flung battle was offstage noise. Back in civilian life, I quite forgot about it until this article gave me an inkling of what had really happened at Leyte Gulf. In crude greatly simplified fact, Halsey had run his immense fleet three hundred miles north-

east, then three hundred miles southwest, and never fired a shot!

On the *Zane* well before that battle, in long night watches passed contemplating starry skies and dark waters, the idea had grown on me that World War II might be something new in the history of man on earth, a clash of all the great nations clear around the planet; and that a novelist might well arise one day and take it on as a sort of global *War and Peace.* Not me, of course! I was then snatching moments to write—despite the nagging captain—another page or two of *Aurora Dawn.* For me this Halsey article was a first passing breeze of the winds of war.

———

The job in hand now was *Marjorie.* Once past the scene with the parents, the scrawls on long yellow pages started to pile up. Marjorie's first horseback ride in Central Park was a low-comedy turn of the funnyman. Prince Charming, a rickety old horse for beginners, bolts with her in an "idiotically enjoyable" gallop, until she tumbles off and lands on the muddy bridle path facedown. New York Jewish collegians are the riding party, and in their reactions—more exactly,

in Marjorie's impression of them—a vein of social painting begins to emerge that would take four years to realize.

The Caine Mutiny Court-Martial

One major interruption ate up many months of those four years.

Sarah and I were spending the summer on Fire Island in a seaside house, a retreat from Manhattan's intrusions. A talked-about novelty, Bernard Shaw's *Don Juan in Hell* came to Broadway, and we went in to see it. The show had toured the country to full houses, a seldom performed third act of *Man and Superman,* in which the Devil traded badinage for two hours with the three leads in Mozart's *Don Juan*: the outraged Donna Anna, the Don, and the Stone Statue that drags him down to Hell. The actors stood or sat at lecterns reading Shaw's lines, and that was the evening's whole entertainment. *"Why can't I do something like this with the court-martial chapters of* Mutiny? *A Broadway show, with little or no effort on my part? It's all written!"* On that lazy mercenary notion, I met with the director Charles Laughton in his hotel suite.

It was my first experience of *The Caine Mutiny* as my calling card.

I cannot describe Charles Laughton here, there was just too much of him. Ugly as sin, inordinately fat, world-famous, triumphant, a terrible flop, Captain Bligh, Quasimodo, Henry Higgins, King Lear, a stooge for a TV puppet, *L'Avare* at the Comédie-Française, Laughton co-produced and directed *Don Juan in Hell*. As the Devil (of course) he had the best lines, and hogged the stage against Don Juan, played by the romantic film idol Charles Boyer. Laughton greeted me in midafternoon in droopy maroon silk pajamas. A waiter brought his breakfast, two double gimlets and bouillabaisse, over which he averred that my *Court-Martial* notion was smashing. He would absolutely love to do it, it just needed a little work: a first act aboard the ship and an editing of my four court-martial chapters to two acts. It is a measure of the man's persuasive force that I went back to Fire Island, set aside *Marjorie,* batted off that first act, and reduced the chapters to two acts, all in a very short time.

Laughton raved about my script, though he observed that on second thought, the first act he had asked for was unnecessary. His co-producer, a young unknown named Paul Gregory, echoed his raves. We

solemnly agreed that the production must never interfere with the writing of *Marjorie Morningstar.* Henry
Fonda met with us, fresh from his long run and Tony
Award in *Mister Roberts,* eager to do my planned
court-martial play either as Captain Queeg or Barney Greenwald. When I told him he was my perfect
Greenwald, he cheerily agreed. The producers went
out to Hollywood to cast the play and start the tour,
and I got back to *Marjorie* for a month or more, with a
surging sense of acceleration.

A week into rehearsal, Gregory telephoned me
from Hollywood. He *hated* to do this, he truly, *truly*
apologized, but the show was running very long in rehearsal. Would I just fly out for a day or two and cut
it? Laughton, he said, was ready to help. I came, and
found Laughton already going at the script. We did
cut the show in half, most of the blood on his scal-
pel. It was now a play that worked. The cast sensed
it in the first run-through; even Henry Fonda, who
had been grousing at everything, was relieved and
happy. I noted an overcut and quietly pointed it out to
Laughton. He seized on it and halted the run-through.
"Gentlemen, the author requests that I give the captain back his balls." The roar of laughter sealed the
upbeat mood of the cast, and I flew back to *Marjorie.*

But not for long. Crisis upon crisis erupted between Fonda and Laughton. Time after time—worst of all in Chicago—I was summoned to "save the show." When it arrived in Boston, the reviews were excellent, the players' mood funereal. Laughton warned me, in the hollow tones of the Stone Statue, that Fonda was unmanageable; they might not open on Broadway at all. On opening night I went backstage before curtain time and found Fonda in the pink, radiating power and confidence. "We're going to *kill* them," he declared, almost prancing with eagerness. So they did. His performance as Barney Greenwald was a flawless cut diamond of courtroom drama. A competent film actor, Lloyd Nolan, swept all the notices as Captain Queeg. As soon as his contract allowed, Fonda withdrew. Show business.

What of my wife in all this? For one thing she was pregnant, which rather preoccupied her; for another, she developed a detestation of Laughton. Penetrating the Brobdingnagian facade, she found a crafty manipulator, and her perception was unerring. He manipulated me over the bouillabaisse, he never did anything else, and I owe him nevertheless my one great Broadway success. I dedicated the play to him and long remained under his spell, to my wife's chagrin.

The Cover of Time

What author would decline that accolade if he could, though it is not optional? John Marquand gave me fair warning. His novels of Boston society had been a succession of number one bestsellers. A scarred veteran, he put it to me bluntly: "They will be waiting for you with cleavers." He was a judge of the Book of the Month Club, furious at the screeners for rejecting *The Caine Mutiny* without letting the judges read it, and he insisted on seeing the *Marjorie* galleys as soon as they were available. In a rare gentlemanly gesture, he visited me at home to assure me that the book was superb, better written than *Caine,* but that I had to brace myself. My Navy book had come in under the radar and caught the critics unawares. Not again!

Preliminary reactions to the galleys were a puzzling mix. My publishers, who had invested nothing in the novel—they had picked it up gratis in their advance for my Navy book—professed enthusiasm. My agent, a panjandrum in the New York book trade, waited two weeks without a word, then came to my apartment to tell me face-to-face that *Marjorie Morningstar* was an indigestible monster of overwriting. If I hadn't written the book, he wouldn't have read it; it had to be cut

by two-thirds; and even then a sale of 75,000 copies, despite the success of *Caine,* would be amazing. He informed me further that the editor of *McCall's,* then the premier women's magazine, had warned him that Wouk should burn this book, forget I had written it, or it would destroy my career.

Then a letter from Calder Willingham, a recent acquaintance, arrived. I will be writing more about Willingham, a quirky Southern novelist then much in vogue. He had read the book in typescript. Never before or since have I received such a letter. "Let us see what we have here," it began. In forty typed pages, Calder assessed *Marjorie Morningstar* start to finish with astute precision. He presumed on our newfound friendship to threaten, "If you listen to your agent and cut this book, I'll never talk to you again." It was, he said, the first major novel about American Jewry.

Into this baffling split of advance verdicts came the cover of *Time.*

Friend reader, I tell you before God that if I could have written my works and left out of my life the small "celebrity" aspect of it, I would have been grateful to my soul, if not to my inborn writer's hunger for praise and recognition. Certainly, landing on the cover of *Time* with a new book must seem to aspiring authors a Grail. Fred Allen once admonished me so: "Herman,

remember this. For every step you take up the ladder of success, you will get a prick from the porcupine of grief," a word to the wise that I heeded too little.

The split in reactions persisted through and long past publication. The faded memories are coming back as I write. In those days reviews could gash my flesh. On publication day, the book review in *The New York Times* dripped gore; on the front page of the Sunday book section, a guarded encomium! Hard upon the *Time* cover story, the *New York Post* printed a week-long series of articles on my wife and me, wielding not so much a cleaver as a switchblade. The editor was a college friend of mine. And so it went. You saw people on the street carrying the novel under an arm, and it led the bestseller lists; but for the naysayers—and they were many and formidable—such things merely confirmed the *Time* cover as a pillory, and my poor Marjorie, pictured behind me, as a Hester Prynne sellout.

Meantime, Charles Laughton was urging me to write a new play; or had I in the files something he could read? I hunted up my three discards of the *Zane* days. With bloodhound instinct he pounced on one nugget I had borrowed from Cervantes: an inserted novella in *Don Quixote* called *The Curious Impertinent,* actually an old tale found in several versions. A

complacent dullard of a husband wagers a friend, Lothario, that he cannot seduce his wife, and Lothario succeeds. I thought my effort a ham-handed misfire. "Oh, no!" Laughton exulted. My Lothario play as it stood was pure French farce, and with a little work it could dazzle Broadway. He sent me the complete works of Molière, Marivaux, Beaumarchais, and all of Georges Feydeau's boulevardier farces. I had never heard of "boulevardier farce" or Feydeau.

I am raveling out a weaved-up folly here. The Lothario play consumed two years of my life, and landed us in the Virgin Islands, so there is no skipping it.

In the book world the *Marjorie* barrage pro and con was dying down, but not in the Jewish press. When I read a long critique in an academic Jewish quarterly by a fellow novelist, headed NOT EVEN TRASH, I decided, Okay, this does it, let's hunker down and start the next book. I'd had the title, *Hawke's Mother,* for years; theme, the death of Balzac in his mother's arms, poignantly limned in Stefan Zweig's biography. My protagonist would be an American, that I always knew. Once I got down to work, Honoré de Balzac and Thomas Wolfe, both literary men of superhuman creative force, and both perpetual mama's boys who died early, would fuse and spring to hot life as the

big bestseller writer from the Kentucky hill country, Arthur Youngblood Hawke.

But this was not to be. Not yet.

The American Molière

One's Broadway hit is a harmless pleasure to revisit now and then. Standing in the back of the theater at *The Caine Mutiny Court-Martial* with Laughton, watching Henry Fonda pulverize a Freudian psychiatrist to gales of laughter in a packed house, I heard a Mephistophelian murmur in my ear, "Herman, that's Molière." The manipulator was now taking hold of my Achilles heel. Being a funnyman was my boyhood dream, remember, not dead but dormant. Molière I knew pretty well, the other classics less so, but Feydeau was new to me, a gold strike. My French was good and got better as I whipped through his brittle fizzy farces, one funnier than the next: *Feu La Mère de Madame, On Purge Bébé, Occupe-toi d'Amélie*: even if one didn't know French, the very titles rolling off Laughton's tongue made one smile. I read the whole Feydeau oeuvre while making my first raw notes on *Youngblood Hawke,* and found myself becoming dis-

tracted and tempted, as I had been by Kurt Weill years ago: fix *The Curious Impertinent* for Broadway now as a boulevardier farce, or work ahead in earnest on the new novel?

Youngblood Hawke was changing form and theme, as I was changing as a man and a writer. The gag-man was gone like my childhood. Propelled by an ill-understood destiny, I had earned some prominence (and envy) as a novelist. When I turned forty, Columbia had put on an exhibit in the Low Memorial Library of my manuscripts, which struck me as decidedly premature; I was just starting *Hawke,* and I was having intimations of a huge book to follow it, a freshening breeze of the winds of war. In my daily diary of the time, there are references to "the main task," and now and then "Gog and Magog." For such a mighty theme, I would have to create a host of characters not Jewish, not admen, not New Yorkers, not destroyer sailors, not even Americans, people entirely outside my own life; and *Youngblood Hawke* was gaining focus as, among other things, a trial run for that main task. In its own right, it would be a fable of a resolute coal-town boy in the big city, a naive powerful author buffeted and ultimately done in by big money, a sophisticated older woman, and his own gross follies.

What was it to be, then: Lothario or *Youngblood*

Hawke? Writers are slippery self-deceivers. Listen to my own logic for handling this dilemma, as I can reconstruct it fifty years later. "Look, *The Curious Impertinent* is written already! Sure, it needs work, but compared to writing the first chapter of *Hawke,* from a cold-iron start? It is to laugh. *Marjorie* turned out a four-year grind, and probably *Hawke* will. I've learned a lot, and I'll proceed with my eyes wide open. I'm entitled to a breather, that's all, a fun thing, bringing Feydeau farce to the jaded Broadway audience. Let's go, it's Lothario!"

The die was cast. And what of my wife, whom Laughton had jocularly dubbed Cerberus? The darling of my days was busy at a yearlong project, redecorating and refurnishing a Park Avenue duplex we had settled into after the *Caine*'s success. (Shades of the Great Neck mansion and the Gag Czar's penthouse!) The fact is, Sarah liked *The Curious Impertinent*. When we were first falling in love she had read it with glassy eyes, and had not looked at it in the years since. So just this once Cerberus failed to bark, and we were headed, all unknowing, down a long gentle slope to the Caribbean.

The Broadway in-crowd—which long ago flew off Fire Island to roost in the Hamptons—in those days frequented the open house in Ocean Beach of

Herman Levin, the producer of *My Fair Lady*. There Sarah and I met Alan Meltzer, a man-about-town often seen at the round front table in Sardi's, amusing stars like Elizabeth Taylor and Truman Capote. Meltzer's métier was getting people's names in the papers. He was quite the raconteur, and that night at Levin's house, telling of his debacle trying to run a hotel on St. Thomas, he was convulsing everyone and laughing wryly at himself. His story struck me as a theme for a novel (a decade later it became my *Don't Stop the Carnival*), and I invited him to my house to talk about it. Next day he poured out the whole tragicomic truth to me, but he demurred at writing a book. We agreed to visit St. Thomas together one day, a vagary I quite forgot.

That summer when I got to work in earnest on the Lothario play, it fell apart in my hands. There was really nothing there, a cobwebbed old tale and a jejune wartime scrawl; but by now I had the bit in my teeth. All winter there had swirled around me the theme for a pristine French farce. My wife had an Achilles heel herself—interior decoration. She was a decorating fool, and with a fashionable decorator at her elbow, she was making the staid duplex newly elegant, smartly styled, and even on budget, but the process was hell on my peace of mind. In the beach

house quiet reigned. While she swept into town and out again, decorating away, I started over in a Feydeau fever. The writing was a breeze. Lothario was gone, and I was making frothy fun of ourselves as parvenus on Park Avenue. I brought a finished draft back into town. Laughton was at first desolate at my dropping Lothario but, after a few days, phoned me to walk with him in Central Park; where, amid the falling leaves, he declared *Nature's Way* a surprising departure, a lovely fresh blending of French style and American wit. With a little more work it would be ready to go, and would be fabulous.

Thus encouraged, I sent it to my agent. He read it, called it a uranium mine, and contacted Leland Hayward, then the leading producer on Broadway. Hayward hungrily asked to read the script, and his response was swift. He wanted *Nature's Way*. He was ready to produce it! My agent excitedly notified his Hollywood co-agent of this. In short order, the co-agent let him know that, sight unseen, two major studios were ready to deal. Leland Hayward then invited me to lunch and praised all my works, especially the new play. Upshot of the lunch, the script needed a few touches, somewhat different from Laughton's ideas. My agent agreed that, on second thought, the play

could indeed use a bit of tailoring. So I started the first of many, many revisions.

———

Well, enough raveling out?

A paperback edition of *Nature's Way* for stock companies, dating back to those days, still offers the play today as "a hilarious and zany romp," and goes on:

> [*It*] *was greeted as an astonishing change of pace for Herman Wouk, author of such serious dramas as* The Caine Mutiny Court-Martial . . . *and the world-famous novels* Marjorie Morningstar *and* The Caine Mutiny. *The New York Times reported that "the audience laughed its head off"; The Philadelphia Bulletin that "the audience was helpless with hysterical laughter"* . . .

All perfectly true.

Nature's Way was one hell of a flop. It ran two months on theater parties, and *finis*. I never heard from Hayward after my first revision. Laughton did phone. Alas, he had to withdraw due to a film offer to play Nero that he couldn't refuse. My agent, nothing

daunted, offered the uranium mine to an esteemed producer, Alfred de Liagre, Jr. At the same time a different agent offered de Liagre a musical called *West Side Story*. He chose to produce *Nature's Way*. (Show business!) Brock Pemberton, a wise old producer, watched *Nature's Way* with me in a half-empty theater resounding with hollow laughter. Said Pemberton, "They laugh, but they don't buy."

Curtain down on the Lothario play and the American Molière.

Rothschild's Clock

My grandfather used to say that Lord Rothschild had a clock that struck the hour by booming, "One Hour Nearer Death!" I have a haunting conscience about wasted time. Not that I haven't wasted staggering amounts of time and still do; only that when I do I am plagued, eaten alive, by guilt. Two years gone from my brief time on earth! Failure was pain enough, but the guilt, the guilt, of two years lost to mere wheedling flattery! Down the duplex incinerator I dumped all files of *Nature's Way,* scripts, correspondence, contracts, multifarious drafts, and rehearsal notes; among

my papers, no trace remains of the uranium mine. Too low to resume *Youngblood Hawke,* I began a piece of busywork to divert my sore spirit, an impulsive bounce-back, which took hold and may outlive all my other writings. In the Fiddler part of this book, I may write more about *This Is My God.* Let me here give it a page or two before we shake the dust of New York from our feet, put Sardi's and Park Avenue behind us forever, and land in the Caribbean for six crazy and marvelously productive years.

My working title, *A Letter to My Nephew,* was the genuine germ of the thing. When the bar mitzvah of my oldest nephew drew near, I planned a long letter to him about the worth and glory of our religion. The bar mitzvah came and went, I did not write the letter, and I quieted my conscience with a resolve to write a short book on the theme someday. In the rebound from the failure, I was just starting that book when a rabid agnostic, my taxman, asked me with a shy grin, "This may surprise you, but can you recommend something about Hanukkah that I can give my son—purely for culture, you understand, not for religion?" I seized on that as my opening sentence. It stands there today. The words started to pour out, but soon they slowed. Did I really propose to write, at this point in my life, a personal account of my Judaism?

The unexpected answer was yes, let's give it a shot. Way back in Great Neck, Sarah and I had encountered suburban Jewish eyebrows raised in amusement at learning we kept kosher. With New York's Broadway and literary Jewish insiders we had clearly "made it," but our ways disconcerted them as well. They saw us and socialized with us at Sardi's, yet we declined their friendly dinner invitations. We were weird mavericks, no question. Christians like Calder Willingham took us quite for granted; it was only Jews who found us odd. (All this was transpiring, remember, in the 1950s. There has since been something of a shift in American-Jewish attitudes.) The challenge was tricky and, the more I thought about it, not trivial. "Do what you feel like doing" has been my rule at work, so I bulled ahead and found myself enjoying a candid pass at describing a faith I loved.

But what a wretched New York winter that was! Snowy, windy, rainy, slushy, dark, *dark!* Both kids were sick by turns, one would miss first grade, then the other preschool. When they were both in health, like as not the weather kept us from taking them to Central Park. What about fresh air? Well, our duplex apartment was in some luxury buildings enclosing a little square of evergreen trees and shrubs, open to the sky. Our boys, bundled up to their noses, would play

in that square, and if a blizzard dumped some snow down the shaft, they could romp in a cramped tiny winter wonderland.

For Sarah and me, a freshly bloodied playwright and his lady, Sardi's was hardly the place to take our ease of an evening. There were new Broadway hits like *West Side Story*—we could have had insiders' tickets—but getting to the theater and back in a cab or a limo, what a weariness of plugged-up side streets, what inch-by-inch crawling! Near our place there was a hotel with an elegant bar to which we resorted just to get out of the duplex at night. The bar was quiet, the martinis excellent, the upscale clientele mostly mature gentlemen with tall beautiful hookers. I was not noticed, but Sarah did draw puzzled glances.

———

Heavy rain beat on my library window as I sat at my desk, scrawling an opening chapter of *A Letter to My Nephew*. A wood fire burned in the working fireplace, a sybaritic but cosy luxury in our third-floor duplex. I was deep in a writing mood, pouring out an early cagey passage about God, when the telephone rang. Reluctantly I picked it up. I barely remembered the man's name: Alan Meltzer, the Broadway press agent,

who had had the hilarious disaster trying to run a hotel in the Caribbean.

"Oh hi there, Alan. What's up?"

"How about next weekend, a quick trip to St. Thomas? Three, four days down and back, all you need to get the picture for a novel . . ."

Next weekend . . . Siegelman bar mitzvah, tickets for the ballet . . . anyway, what a drag, stopping work, clearing it with Sarah, packing, battling the JFK mobs . . . "Alan, thanks for calling, but right now I can't—"

Cheerily: "Well, first of next month?"

Hmm. I put God aside to think. A truthful, funny, sad, disastrous misadventure in an island paradise: not a bad notion, some day. Meantime, a bit of Caribbean sunshine . . . "Thanks for remembering, Alan. Can I call you back? I'd really like to do this . . ."

CHAPTER THREE

The Main Task I

Island Fever

SARAH AND I SIT in webbed lounge chairs outside a rented cottage high above the U-shaped sweep of Magens Bay, a purple-blue arm of the sea that shades to green shallows and a long uninhabited white beach. The year is 1957. What Magens Bay looks like today, I have no idea, and am glad I do not. She holds in her lap the manuscript of *A Letter to My Nephew* and is saying, "I don't like it. If you hadn't written it, I wouldn't have gone on reading it. You're just making the best of a committed position." Many months later, still in that little cottage, I show her a total rewrite

called *The Intelligent Skeptic's Guide to the Jewish Religion.* "Better," she says: all I need from her, but that title is an unseemly crib from George Bernard Shaw.*
Around then a Talmudist friend visits, reads the manuscript, and voices cool approval with a learned quote: "I guess it's your way of saying, 'This is my God, and I will praise Him.' "†

Aha . . .

My agent in New York receives the script of *This Is My God.* In a long-distance call, he has trouble with "Judaism." He calls it *Juduism,* then *Judiasm,* and he forwards the script without comment to Doubleday. The publisher, obviously disconcerted by this religious aberration of a bestselling author, orders a first printing of a few thousand copies, counting on readers of my novels to absorb them. *This Is My God* skyrockets off, taking second place in nonfiction sales for half a year to the playwright Moss Hart's lively memoir, *Act One.* Amid the scattered reader letters that reach me on St. Thomas, there comes one from Isidore Epstein in London, editor of the English translation of the Soncino Talmud. *This Is My God,* he writes, is the

---

The Intelligent Woman's Guide to Socialism and Communism.
†Exodus 15:2 (Holy Bible, New Living Translation).

best book he knows on the theme, and the first in English.

———

The craziest part of our Caribbean interlude was building a house. We went house-hunting but found none that suited us, so we built one on a choice mountain site with stunning views of both the Atlantic and the Caribbean, and a stunning price tag to match. I pass over the drawn-out comic costly horrors of dealing with island contractors and architects; it is all in *Don't Stop the Carnival*. We called the place Star Pines, after the trees that grew on the site. We dwelled in Star Pines for three or so years, then put it up for sale and returned to the U.S.A. to live. An indulgence, Star Pines, not to say a lunacy? Well, maybe. Then again, shortly before we fled New York, we dined in the Dakota, an old ultra-exclusive apartment building on Central Park West, called by insiders just "Dakota." A nice Jewish dramatist, who had recently made it into Dakota, beseeched us to come and dine with him, promising us tuna salad on new plates. In the dark wood-paneled dining room, we found ourselves at a round table lined with strictly in-crowd guests,

under a spectacular movable chandelier right out of *The Phantom of the Opera,* in which perhaps fifty tall sepulchral candles flamed. Choose your lunacy. We built Star Pines, where I wrote *Youngblood Hawke.*

Calder and Youngblood

The longest of all my works, it is actually based on my twelve years after the Navy when I struck it rich as a novelist, a Sinbad voyage on a flying carpet of marketable talent through publishing, Hollywood, and Broadway. My carpet crashed and burned, as the reader knows, in the Laughton uranium mine. In the novel the play is *The Lady from Letchworth,* Laughton is called Georges Feydal, and the crash kills Young-blood Hawke.

I could not have written this novel without knowing Calder Willingham. By disguising myself as a novelist from the Deep South, and presumptuously touching in color from the great Thomas Wolfe's short tragic life, I could romance as I pleased about those twelve years, making up names for the real people and—by instinct—reaching out for a new panoramic style of fiction: far-ranging counterplots, including a legal bat-

tle over coal land, a slippery real estate adviser who traps Hawke in crushing tax trouble, and a congressional investigation into communism, all tied together by the author's love affairs, cliff-hanging finances, and tough litigious mother.

When we met by chance Calder was "the novelist" to the life—worn duffel coat, shock of flaming red hair, gaunt pallid freckled face—as compared to my dull synagogue-going uptown look; yet that same day we ended up in his cellar pad in the Village, talking royalties and competitors. We were fellow outsiders in the New York literary game, that was our bond. Calder's narrative style, flawless lucid prose with a savage comic streak, was unfashionably easy to read, whereas I was bearing with fortitude my disgrace as a *Time*-cover sellout. Calder had a maniacal self-confidence in his talent, alternating with despair. His first novel won major reviews, hailing him as an important new Southern voice. His second book incurred Marquand's cleavers, and his sales stopped dead. He went to Hollywood perforce for his bread, and doggedly wrote his novels while working on top films.* His mercurial temperament, alas, got him

---

* *Paths of Glory, Patton, Bridge over the River Kwai, Little Big Man, The Graduate.*

thrown off the set more than once, and even denied screen credit. He was the only novelist with whom I ever exchanged work in progress, my one trusted fellow author. His name stands today in Southern fiction as an unjustly neglected comic prose master.

"You Have to Go to Germany"

Scrawling at *Youngblood Hawke* on a favorite breezy spot looking north to the Atlantic and south to the Caribbean (when I looked, which was seldom) I was absorbed in the fortunes of my composite hero, who had come alive on the first page, drawling, *"Mah one vass,"* pulling from his shabby jacket a leather case of dollar cigars and lighting one with assumed calm, as he faced an editor over his huge untidy first novel on the desk. Star Pines was my best place to write, ever. The pages had piled up, I had a book-length script in hand, yet I felt the story was just getting started; and I was driving ahead with gusto when my wife came and handed me a magazine open to a book review, saying, "You're going to write about Europe."

An arresting remark! She knew the main task far ahead was to be centered on Admiral Halsey's fiasco at

Leyte—working title, *The Gulf*—expanded in scope and depth to epitomize the folly of industrialized war. The reviewer was British historian Hugh Trevor-Roper, author of *The Last Days of Hitler,* a notable success, and he was extravagantly praising *The Destruction of the European Jews* by one Raul Hilberg. Sarah did not explain herself. She seldom did. Perhaps she thought I was bound to touch on the European side of the war, and should read this account of what happened to the Jews. Not a bad notion, at that; I sent for the book. When it arrived, the volume at first glance was not inviting: obscure publisher, cheap binding, a thick book printed in two columns to a page, a nuisance to read.

The Destruction of the European Jews changed my main task once and for all. It is a mighty twentieth-century masterpiece. It will never be a book for the many, it is too long, heavy, and dark; but the light it sheds on the human condition ensures its survival among the thoughtful few. When I finished it I wrote to the author, asking if I might visit him at the University of Vermont, where he was an assistant professor. After this visit, because of what I learned from Hilberg, I was able many years later to write *The Winds of War* and *War and Remembrance.* Those novels might not exist otherwise.

Raul Hilberg was a reticent man, dour and difficult

to know. He nevertheless responded to my approach with chill brilliance, possibly because he believed that I grasped his work. In a day of long walks on the university grounds, I described my "main task." Writing it was no longer possible, I told him, unless I could make the substance of his book part of my story; but of that I despaired, because it happened on the other side of the planet, in another war. He listened in silence to my long anxious harangue. When I stopped talking, he did not respond for a while. Then he said, "You've got to go to Germany."

It was a shocker. I said I had resolved never to set foot in Germany while I lived.

"I know, I know. You've got to go to Germany."

He opened up about his own work. It had originated in his master's thesis on the Jews under the Nazis. His mentor, a Columbia social science professor, like him a Jewish refugee from Nazi Europe, had written a well-regarded book on National Socialism; and he warned Hilberg against expanding his thesis on the Jewish fate to a published book. The subject was shunned and repellent, he said, and could only damage his academic career. In any case, as it stood the material needed a structure. This mentor had drummed "structure" into Hilberg, who resolved to go ahead with the book, structuring it on the Germans,

the perpetrators of the massacre, not on the victims. That was the key decision.

Hilberg and I talked back and forth about how to structure a novel encompassing two different wars in two hemispheres. Of course, there was no solving the problem in a ramble around the university. I brought two things away with me for the main task: I had to go to Germany, and I had to find a structure.

Hilberg was dead right, of course, about Germany. The movie nightmare land of heel-clicking uniformed sadists and comic bumbling boobs bore no resemblance whatever to the Germany that Sarah and I encountered, a lovely country much like France or England, the people not unlike Americans. *The Caine Mutiny* (*Die Caine war ihr Schicksal*) had made me famous there. I visited an eminent "good German" politician, Franz Josef Strauss, at his home overlooking the Rhine River, then at flood. My first words to him were "What happened?" His genial cordiality gave way to a drawn grave look. He gestured out of the window at the roaring Rhine, and sadly shrugged.

My publisher, a merry little gentleman named Wolfgang Kruger, and his starchy wife treated Sarah and me with the awed respect due a great writer, and for a little light fun took us to the Reeperbahn, the red-light district of Hamburg, where respectable folk

like themselves watched comely strippers undress and gyrate. A friendly journalist took us in tow, a tall blue-eyed blond-haired fellow, Aryan to his long straight nose. For two days he brought us here and there wherever we asked, including a mass grave and a crematorium, anxiously trying all the time to assure us that "it" was absolutely over. Indeed, on the whole it seemed to be. His last plea, shouted to us as we were boarding our plane to go home, was "You can't indict a whole people." The Eichmann trial was imminent; the Mossad had nabbed him in Argentina. At that time, "holocaust"—with a small "h"—still meant a burnt sacrifice or a widespread destructive fire. All these impressions are quite fragmentary and out-of-date, to be sure, but the visit did give me a much-needed glimpse of real live Germans.

Writing about Raul Hilberg has irresistibly brought to mind Dan Gallery, the first admiral I ever encountered man-to-man. In 1951, when *The Caine Mutiny* first came out, the reaction in the Navy was, in a word, "Harumph!" A fan letter I got from one Rear Admiral Daniel Gallery—"best novel I've ever read about the modern Navy"—was a reassuring jolt, marking him a maverick. So he proved. He asked that we meet, and it turned out that he wanted something. He had sold some short stories to *The Saturday Evening Post* and

needed a literary agent. I suggested my own agent, and so began a friendship fully as crucial to my war novels as encountering Hilberg and his book, if not more so; though Gallery's importance took shape only when we returned to the mainland.

Interlude

Time in the tropics just slides by. Elsewhere leaves fall, sweaters come out or fold away, foods and drinks vary with the seasons, and it can snow. On Star Pines, none of that went. One needed a calendar if time mattered. For our boys it was always summertime. I was driving head-down through an endless book. My enigmatic wife grilled lunches on one or another almost deserted beach, with ice-cold martinis from vacuum jars; she most enjoyed our night forays to Katie's, a bar where Katie, a fat lesbian piano player with a mischievous eye, played old Broadway scores to all hours. We chartered sailboats and with luck saw whales. At an exhausted halt in Hawke's complicated downfall, I switched to a funny novel about Meltzer, which languished after a few pages. I caught my breath and lurched to the end of the endless novel. We had been on St. Thomas for five years.

"The New Wouk" (ex *"Hawke's Mother"*)

The beating heart of *Youngblood Hawke* is a disastrous love story that frames his meteoric twelve-year rise and crash. In the first chapter he meets Jeanne Green, a fetching California career girl working for the publisher as a stylist. In the second chapter he encounters Mrs. Frieda Winter, a Manhattan woman of fashion, at a lavish Christmas party in the publisher's home. Hawke is chatting with her and young Jeanne, when Mrs. Winter puts down the girl with a poisonous compliment about her hat. Jeanne feels the gibe to her bones; Hawke is oblivious to it. That swiftly passing moment foreshadows the story. Jeanie Green is a full-length portrait of my wife. We never once spoke of this to each other, but Arthur Hawke's life is my nightmare vision of what might well have become of me, had we not met and loved.

That was not how the novel was perceived on publication. My agent sold the magazine rights at a big noised-about price to the same editor who had told him that I should burn *Marjorie Morningstar.* His co-agent in Hollywood made a swift pre-publication deal, and the Book of the Month Club featured "the new Wouk." A New York columnist dubbed *Youngblood*

Hawke "the novel that made a million dollars before publication." The hyperbole went viral, and the voice of the whetstone was heard in the land. Off on a tropical island, trying to get a handle on the main task, I well knew that the money was rolling in, that our insensate squandering on Star Pines was being made up; but I was preoccupied with getting *Gog and Magog* started at last, in my chronic race against Rothschild's clock. *Youngblood Hawke* landed high on the bestseller lists, though not soaring off: a letdown, yet after all much in the way of nature. A bit of a shock, though, was the news that merry little Herr Wolfgang Kruger was declining the German rights. It took me down a peg, no doubt for the good of my soul.

Time to start writing pages, if the main task was not to be a lifelong self-comforting delusion! Right off I needed, for Hilberg's structure, a leading Jewish character to carry the European part of the story. Bernard Berenson, an art historian, came to mind: a converted Jew—in fact a Litvak like my family—who became wealthy authenticating Renaissance paintings. Berenson dwelled outside Florence in his luxurious villa, I Tatti, and there he stayed all during World War II, strangely unmolested by Mussolini's anti-Semitic laws, and even by the ruthless Germans when they occupied Italy. How had he remained so pecu-

liarly safe through it all? Connections? Bribes? Sheer good fortune? It happened, and gave me my chief European figure, Aaron Jastrow, though that would not be his name for a long while.

Thinking of Berenson, truth to tell, deeply discouraged me about the whole vast project at the outset. "The *Gulf*?" I was utterly nowhere. How could that old lapsed Jew outside Florence conceivably be made to fit with "Bull" Halsey and the great sea fight off Leyte? *What was my story?* Of what use was my head full of military thinking, from Sun Tzu to Liddell Hart? Such were my agonized misgivings in the backwash of five years of literary toil on an ill-regarded book. One afternoon Sarah and I were at Morningstar Beach sipping rum punches at the open-air bar, the boys were frolicking in and out of the surf in the sunshine, white folk like us were dancing in a ring to a calypso record, and I asked myself, "Is *this* where we intend to live out our lives?"

As *Youngblood Hawke* sank on the lists, it occurred to me that the congressional hearings on communism in the book—somewhat like the court-martial in *The Caine Mutiny*—might just make a fine Broadway play. I had done the research. The thing was sound and dramatic. Why not try it? Very tentatively, I broached the notion to BSW. She turned on me, as only she

could. "WHAT! You haven't yet sat shiva on *Young-blood Hawke,* and you're ready to pull it apart and use a piece? What is it you don't want to write?" (Shiva, meaning "seven," is a week of mourning, when Jews sit on low stools to receive condolences.)

"The big war book. I'm not ready for it."

"Well, then, write the Meltzer book."

So I did. It took another year. When we arrived stateside, my typescript of *The Caribbean Comedy* was ready to go, and my thinking on the War Book was much advanced. Berenson was now a Yale history professor named Mendelssohn who had hit the Book of the Month Club with a bestseller called *A Jew's Jesus,* and had retired to Italy on the proceeds, with a niece as companion and secretary. How he related to Admiral Halsey, I still had not the ghost of an idea.

Sarah and I never gave returning to New York a second thought. Boston would be best for universities, San Francisco for the good life, Washington for research, so we sorted it out. Washington it was, and in time we would find there the good life and the universities, too. We arrived late in 1964 and rented a handsome house on buzzing Massachusetts Avenue, where I wrote the first words of the big War Book. "*I am stateless.*" Professor Mendelssohn was himself starting a book, a sequel to *A Jew's Jesus.* He had no title, and

not much of an idea. His American publisher wanted a sequel, so he meant to provide one. Under the professorial patina he was a canny Jew, much like Berenson under the art historian . . .

All at once, I found myself co-opted to write brochures for Lyndon Johnson's inauguration! The co-chairmen of the committee—a famed Washington lawyer and a New York theater mogul who managed the Kennedy Center—commandeered me. How could I say no? It was my first taste of the way eminent people in Washington use other people. My words were snapped up as I wrote them and printed on creamy paper. We received invitations for more elite inaugural parties than we could accept. Sarah had worked in Navy personnel in wartime Washington, a California Phi Bete scraping along on meager pay; now a lady of means, she plunged zestfully into the exclusive shops for the latest elegant mainland duds. Despite new heavy coats, still thin-blooded from the tropics, we shivered in bitter cold, sitting in front-row seats for the inaugural address. The president-elect spoke from a White House balcony in just a business suit and (I could have sworn) thermal underwear. That night we were shepherded all over town to dances and parties, ending up at the Inaugural Ball, a dazzling phantasmagoria. Among the great of the nation, I danced

with the love of my life, nearly bumping into the President and his wife, a huge man and a little lady.

One memory of this odd swift passage will be with me until I die. In an almost empty anteroom where I sat alone while BSW freshened up, the President entered with two advisers and sat down to read a long dispatch. From his mien, I surmised that it was from Vietnam, and bad. Lyndon Johnson happened once to glance up and meet my look. The cold veiled eyes of a master politician scared me.

First order of business in Washington: *get in touch with Gallery!* Retired to his home in Oakton, Virginia, he had been writing full-time, making good money on the books and stories he sent me for comment. Daniel Gallery would be my Pacific lead in *The Gulf,* no contest. As a guest aboard his aircraft carrier, I had seen him in action: distant, cold-blooded, tough, getting things done with few words. Victor "Pug" Henry in the two-volume saga is—and is not, to be sure—Daniel Gallery. In my man there is none of the contrarian Gallery, who in wartime was called an "original" by the hard-bitten Admiral King, not exactly a compliment. My Pug Henry could not have voiced the "revolt of the admirals" in magazine articles, defying the Defense Department's unification plan to abolish the Marine Corps and shrink the Navy. Nor, indeed, for that mat-

ter, would Victor Henry have written to praise me for *The Caine Mutiny*. He might have enjoyed the story, but would have regretted that a "Captain Queeg" (he had done his time under such!) was spotlighted in a popular novel.

With some diffidence, I telephoned the retired admiral to ask whether I could come out to Oakton to discuss a book I was working on. He showed up instead at my rental house in an hour or so. We sat in facing armchairs, and he heard me out much as Raul Hilberg had done, not commenting until I stopped talking. After some questions about my main character, he observed, "Well, you could send him as the naval attaché to Berlin." It was a radical shift, something to think about. He told me, when I asked him, that he was writing another "Fatso" about a chief gunner's mate who got in and out of salty scrapes, surefire magazine stuff. Dan was working Fatso pretty hard.

The attaché idea grew on me. My Pacific officer had to rise to flag rank, then serve at Leyte in a high command, probably as a vice admiral. Much earlier, he had to come to President Roosevelt's attention as a useful anonymous officer. Gallery himself was too "original," as King had put it. I had diagrammed my character as a toned-down Daniel Gallery with a submariner son and a flighty wife, but he was not alive.

At that time—and I adduce this because it is the truth—I was reading a Trollope novel, *Nina Balatka,* the story of a good Christian girl who loved a Jew. Why and how that struck a spark, I do not pretend to know. The spark flew. The inert diagram blazed up. The submariner son, Byron Henry, would meet and fall in love with Mendelssohn's Jewish niece in Italy; and with his father in Germany as attaché, the whole story could start to roll.

I wrote an opening scene about the man and his family, a second draft, a third; hopeless stuff I thought, but let Gallery tell me so! Payback time for Dan Gallery! I sent the draft to him. The day he received it he phoned and came into town. He wanted to object, vehemently and at some length, to the father's letter to his son about the Jewish girl. "I don't like the fellow," said Gallery. "I don't believe him. That letter offends me." Gallery was a solid Christian, a practicing Catholic. Had I really struck such a false note? After all, Gallery had so nearly accepted my invented Henry family that the letter had gored him. Good enough! I rewrote the letter. It stands as rewritten today, word for word, at the end of Chapter One in *The Winds of War.*

With that, I was off on an arduous seven-year run (or so I calculated) to execute the main task. We moved three times in those seven years, settling down

at last by buying an 1815 Federal row house, three blocks from the Georgetown synagogue. Through all the moving, and despite the heady Georgetown social scene, I piled pages on pages. Characters came swarming into the story, most importantly Byron's brother, Warren. I created Warren Henry to die at the Battle of Midway.

Adding a brother for Byron to a huge book already started was a very close call. It meant further expanding the novel to a size hard to imagine or control. A shadowy older brother to get shot down at Midway would not have done it. No, Warren Henry had to have his authentic persona as a Navy aviator: his Annapolis record, his strengths and weaknesses, his women, his goals, his flying skills, all alien territory to me. Still more research! Well, forward then. Tell the tale, hold your audience, take your chances, and peace to "the few blear-eyed fellows," as Erasmus laughed off his scholastic scolds. I had come to understand World War II as in reality the first global war. (And God grant, the last.) In early 1942 the Battle of Midway, though in itself not decisive, deflected the grim course of defeat after defeat in the colossal planetary conflict, toward the far-off global victory in 1945. The reader, I decided, had to be there at Midway. I called Byron's brother to life.

CHAPTER FOUR

The Main Task II

"DON'T TELL ME YOU bought the purple house!" Georgetown acquaintances would exclaim at first. The previous owner, an eccentric spinster, had so empurpled it throughout that it had been on the market for years, unsalable.* Sarah's decorative demon awoke. We bought the place, and she was in the racketing upheaval of restoring it when my writing stopped dead. I moved out to seek peace in a room at the Cosmos Club. One evening I came home for dinner, and

---

* Full disclosure: there was also the matter of a floor that had fallen through.

I was reading my day's work to her afterward amid the disorder, when she burst out, "You can't do that!" A German general, writing in prison, was explaining that Hitler's invasion of Poland had all been England's fault. "Who *is* this general? You *can't* stop the story dead like that! He doesn't even *sound* German. What are you thinking?"

I tried to explain that the big war book wasn't working, that my plan to scatter characters around the world to convey the global aspect (my first Hilberg's "structure") was in collapse. She did not understand. I could not make her understand. I could only say in desperation, "Look, I do this or I quit." That she understood, grumbling, "Oh, don't quit." Down the years she had seen me back out of many a narrative blind alley. Now I had to grope my way out of this one.

In point of fact, I had groped my way forward into Hilberg's structure! The grand narrative scheme that would carry me through so many years of war writing had at last come in sight. I was a while getting the general straight. At first he was "General von Goethe" (a Princeton historian had to talk me out of that), and he was a jarring intruder, not in any way related to the story, for Victor Henry as his translator was a later idea. Yet if I had to submit to a court of angels a sample of my stuff, it might well be General Armin von Roon.

Only in his retrospect on the global war, written in prison during twenty years of enforced leisure—a former insider in Hitler's entourage, a professional soldier with strong informed judgments on all the campaigns including the Pacific sea fights—only so, I say, could the story structure come clear as the brightly lit drama of the Henrys and the Jastrows, played out against the dark cyclorama of General Armin von Roon's military history.

Byron Henry, the hero of the central love story, is a good-looking charming loafer, a drifter, a do-nothing who slides along the low track in life, barely passing examinations or, if they don't matter that much, flunking them. He goes not to Annapolis but to Columbia. The only subject that interests him at Columbia is a known gut course for athletes, art history. The easygoing old professor discerns quality in Byron and befriends him, which fires Byron up to pursue a master's degree in Florence, but he gets bored and drops it. His mentor then sends him a letter of introduction to Professor Jastrow in Siena, where he encounters Jastrow's niece Natalie.

Within a few pages we find Byron Henry in a small Polish town, utterly transformed: a leaping bounding Gentile in a yarmulke, joining a wild wedding dance of bearded Jews young and old, while Natalie cavorts

with the dancing women. The bridegroom is the son of Professor Jastrow's cousin Berel Jastrow, and this shtetl is their birthplace, where when they were boys they had been yeshiva buddies. Hitler has declared war on Poland, the Germans have already invaded, but the hinterland does not yet have the word. Bright and early next morning Byron, heavily asleep on the floor in the rabbi's house, is shaken awake by Berel Jastrow, a tall Jew with a long brown beard. "De Chormans," he says.

"The Germans?" Byron is up like a cat. "What about them?"

"Dey comink."

———

It is Natalie Jastrow's doing, of course, that has Byron Henry capering at an old-time Jewish wedding in the Polish countryside. Natalie is a hard charger, headstrong and heedless, working for her uncle in Siena just to be near a Rhodes scholar, Leslie Slote—now a Foreign Service officer in Warsaw—with whom she has been having a turbulent on-and-off affair. Storm clouds are gathering in August 1939 when she drags Byron with her in a harebrained excursion to Warsaw to pursue Leslie Slote. Her uncle lets her go only be-

cause Byron agrees to accompany her. So the reader too is dragged, as it were, into the siege of Warsaw, where Byron shows a trace of his father's mettle, performing feats of endurance and bravery that he shrugs off as fun. His thick-skinned insouciance under bombardment both repels and attracts Natalie. Callow though Byron is, and lovesick though she remains for the preoccupied Slote, the Henry mettle catches her eye.

Thus the tale is launched, moving forward to Berlin, Warsaw, Italy, Washington, and the Pacific, at key points thundering ahead with von Roon interpolations. Berel Jastrow gradually comes forward, an indomitable man of faith who grows and grows until in *War and Remembrance* he all but takes center stage.

———

I woke from a seven-year creative trance, as it were, to tell my wife that it was time to submit the manuscript for publication. Her sensible response was "How can you? The story is just beginning." I said jocosely that if I started to write the rest now, I would have to publish a novel with wheels on it. My Doubleday editor suggested usable ways to tie off the incomplete story, pending the writing of a second book; but he thought

Armin von Roon was a mistake, and he seemed bearish about the whole thing. I went to talk to him in New York and found him in a smaller office, no window. On the Meltzer book, final title *Don't Stop the Carnival,* he had missed errors in book design, had not fought the ugly jacket, and the publisher had rushed the novel into print to meet a book club schedule. Now my agent conveyed a perfunctory offer for my war books that amounted to a turndown. As to why Doubleday so acted, I may offer my surmise in the Fiddler part of this book. Here I write of my adventures in the narrative art, and as in the sundial motto, "I tell only sunny hours." (Well, by and large sunny.)

In those days there was, in the book business, a dwindling breed of gentleman publishers who relied on editors rather than marketers in buying and promoting new books. My agent largely redeemed himself by steering me to Arthur Thornhill Jr. of Little, Brown. I flew to Boston to meet his editor in chief, Larned Bradford; and in short, having read the *Gulf* script, Bradford strongly recommended to Thornhill that he publish my war works. Writing the next book took another seven years, and Thornhill stood by his editor's judgment to see the enormous novel through to success. Let me here record my respects to the memory of Ned Bradford, the editor, and Arthur Thornhill

Jr., the publisher, who together shepherded my Main Task to the light of day.

———

Calder Willingham, who wrote me the best letter about *Marjorie Morningstar* that I ever received, now wrote me the worst letter about *The Winds of War* that I ever received. True, it most accurately predicted the novel's early reception by critics, but I had expected better of old Calder. He found my script uninteresting, empty, old-timey, hard to read. His single editorial comment was that Victor Henry's wife, Rhoda, was "a thing to stick pins into," not another word about the Henry family; nothing about the Jastrows, nothing about von Roon, nothing about the portraits of the historical characters: Roosevelt, Churchill, Hitler, Mussolini, not a word! The letter is now filed in a warehouse with the yellowing correspondence of other days. Months later he came to see me bringing a big wooden turtle, my totem, with a brass plaque on it: "To Herman Wouk, the fastest turtle in the west." Such was the gracious wry retraction of a Southern gentleman. I'm not sure Calder ever grasped, or at least conceded, that historical romance was not a dodo literary form. Our friendship lasted until he died.

———

A month to go, and still no title! *The Gulf* was just a working title, and I had not yet thought of another. I was leafing through my work journal and my eye caught a line or two, something like, "just a family story, but the winds of war sweeping through it may give it some . . ." At that moment the telephone rang. My British publisher, Billy Collins, had bought the novel through my agent's London associate and was calling for an update. "Do you have a title yet?"

"Well, I don't know, what would you say to *The Winds of War?*"

"Eh, eh, *what?* What's that?" A gasp, "STROKE OF GENIUS!" That is exactly how it happened. Ned Bradford, delighted and much relieved by the title, invited me a few days later to come and look at a proposed jacket. I found the staid Boston publishing firm a-fizz, and a cover that was, for a book of mine, something new in dignity and beauty. He disclosed over lunch at his haunt, the famed old Locke-Ober restaurant, that the first printing would be a hundred thousand copies. What a dizzying swing up from the Calder letter!

I had trouble getting to sleep the night before publication day. Seven years of work on the line . . . The morning light brought three early reviews: the *New*

York Times daily book column, the advance *Times* Sunday book section, and *Time* magazine.

Next day, the Sabbath, I sat in the synagogue plunged in despair. I had taken Thornhill's money to write another, even longer book that nobody would read! Monday morning I phoned Ned Bradford. Advance orders had stopped at forty thousand, with some returns. "The usual thing, we just sit tight," said Ned cheerily. He thought the reviews weren't bad at all.

My wife more or less agreed with him, but did not argue when I decided to go and sit tight in a cabana on St. Maarten. Star Pines was long since sold. We passed a tense time in retrograde island idleness: sailing, sunning, swimming, dancing, drinking. One morning, a call from the office: telegram for me at the desk, also a letter. I found penciled on a scrap of yellow paper (telegrams came to the island by phone): "Over one hundred thousand ordered and shipped. Ned." The three-page letter was from the novelist Jan de Hartog: * *The Winds of War* was a breakthrough for me, a new thing in current literature, and so on.

---

* A popular Dutch novelist and playwright, who switched to writing in English, living with his wife on a houseboat. His Broadway hits were *The Four Poster* and the musical version, *I Do! I Do!*

Returning to Georgetown, we found sales and reviews tending away from Calder toward de Hartog.

That was the turn. I was sixty-one. Rothschild's clock was striking a late hour.

In *The Winds of War* America is at peace, President Roosevelt candidly rooting for England, and pushing Lend-Lease through a balky Congress torn between isolationists and interventionists, while marchers outside the White House carry placards and shout slogans for both views. *War and Remembrance* picks up the story at Pearl Harbor, and we are in the war up to our necks.

———

The main task I had set for myself was to bring the Holocaust to life in a frame of global war. Here now was the frame, *"the great globe itself,"* and here was the Task itself. The Russians had borne the brunt of Hitler's assault on civilization. Research could do only so much; extensive travel had to be part of the job, starting with the Soviet Union. Sarah and I traveled in that bleak miserable dictatorship for two months: no fun at all, but fully as compulsory as going to Germany had been. We went twice to Auschwitz. We visited Terezin (Theresienstadt), the Czech locale of

the "Paradise Ghetto." In Iran we managed to go to Tehran, where Stalin, Roosevelt, and Churchill met and forged the grand alliance that won the war; and we saw the three embassies where it all happened. We traveled the track of Natalie Jastrow, fleeing a German SS pursuer with her baby and her uncle, down from Siena to the ferry to Corsica, and from there by ship to Marseilles; all this while I wrote a novel more than a thousand pages long.

When Ned Bradford read the typescript he soberly commented, "Herman, this novel was a religious obligation, wasn't it? *The Winds of War* was just a warm-up." There was an editor for you. In my own mind, *Winds* was, and has remained, the pedestal, *Remembrance* the Memorial.

———

Meantime, an unlikely brief glory had opened up in American popular art: a twelve-year window when cable channels were few, the three major networks had the airwaves to themselves, and they fell to battling for ratings with long spectacular films they called "miniseries." Into that window *The Winds of War* lucked, and with a lot more luck, so did the Memorial. Encouraged by my wife, I ventured on

this once-in-a-lifetime shot and ended up writing the screenplays myself, ensuring that at least the history was accurate and the plot and characters true to my books. The two huge movies commanded world audiences; today, viewed on reruns or played at home on disks, they remain in robust life for those who do not enjoy reading long novels.

And here is how all that came about. I was immersed in writing the tragic last chapters of the new book, as usual ignoring commercial TV as a trivial waste of time, when Barry Diller, then the head of ABC, and Michael Eisner, his associate, came to our Georgetown home to try to buy the television rights to *The Winds of War.* Sarah was now virtually my agent, hence this odd house call to negotiate. She and I had resolved, when *Winds* became a bestseller, that the film rights would never be for sale; the scope and the truths of the book were far too serious for the Hollywood meddling that my earlier novels had undergone. On this we had been adamant. The television rights were doubly unthinkable, given the commercial interruptions; nevertheless, after *Roots,* Diller's twelve-hour blockbuster miniseries, the format was red-hot, and they had come to persuade us to think again.

"What do you want?" Diller asked.

"No commercials," Sarah said.

Diller patiently explained that the budget would be far too huge to be spent just for prestige, ABC had to make money. We cited a short NBC miniseries called *Holocaust,* in which commercials for laxatives, feminine hygiene products, even the Ronald McDonald clown had fouled the tragedy. The notion emerged of a short list of prestigious sponsors that we might approve. Sarah did not reject the proposal outright, and they left on an upbeat note, Diller saying at the door, "Well, you've got the power. It's a challenge, anyway." Money was not mentioned, since he had long been offering us increasing sums for those rights in vain.*

Enter Charles "Cy" Rembar, my literary lawyer. It was Cy who had suggested that Sarah become my literary agent when my agent retired. Himself an able author on law, Cy backed up her negotiating instinct with his publishing know-how; they made a tough duo, coping with the treacherous intricacies of Hollywood dealing. Beside the slippery question, "which sponsors?" there was the difficulty in defining exactly what we wanted in faithfulness to plot, characters, and history. When Cy was through with that element,

---

* The offers had been urged on us with ever greater intensity by the late Swifty Lazar, my sometime film agent who shows up in two of my other novels as "Jazz Jacobson" and "Ferdie Lax."

no character could so much as kiss another unless it was there in the book.

Then there were straightforward decisions. Who would write the films, who direct, who produce? Again we had luck which today looks like providence, in a veteran producer and director, Dan Curtis. Dan had created a groundbreaking daytime vampire series, *Dark Shadows,* and was noted for producing adapted horror classics like *Dracula* and *The Turn of the Screw* on time and on budget. He was Jewish, and passionate about the Holocaust. We asked for a British TV writer, Jack Pulman, who had done an excellent serialized *War and Peace,* and in London I conferred with him on the history for a month; but he had scarcely gotten to work when he sickened and died of heart failure. Sarah said that rather than start over with someone else, I had better take on the writing myself. With Dan Curtis's guidance and help, I did my best. Years later, when *The Winds of War* ratings hit a record high, Diller acquired the TV rights to *War and Remembrance,* and much the same contract governed that far grander production, which in 1988 shut the window for good. Cable TV had by then fragmented the audience; yet Curtis's masterly mounting of the 25-hour global panorama held most viewers and won an Emmy, the Oscar of TV.

So much for the irruption of television into my literary life, two years off and on during the sixteen years of the Main Task. No regrets! The cushion of those earnings has enabled me to publish books at five-to-ten-year intervals under no pressure, right down to this book, which I had better get on with.

———

Sequels seldom match the first book's success, all the trade knows that. Here was a book longer than the first, heavier with history, darkened by stern Holocaust realities. A month before publication in 1983, I decamped to Israel with my wife. Newspapers in those days did not reach Israel on pub date, nor did Internet news exist. *Time* magazine did arrive, and BSW picked up a copy in the hotel lobby. "Grudging, grudging," she said, handing it to me. Ned Bradford sent a telegram of congratulations. I had never asked him about the advance printing, and he had not mentioned sales. When we changed planes in London on the way home, I telephoned him at last, and he assured me that things were going "swimmingly." In fact, the novel had a remarkably quick rise in the marketplace, maintained that momentum well into the next year, and with *The Caine Mutiny,* is generally regarded as my best work.

Graham Greene once observed that after sixty, a novelist writes only for money or for fun. At sixty-eight, however, I had not the slightest sense that I was through with the serious stuff. When Sarah and I visited Ned Bradford in Boston to savor the success, I told him I had two more books I wanted to write before I died: an autobiographical novel and a novel about Israel's wars. "Oh, the Israel book by all means," he said. "It's expected of you." As we talked about it, he calmly reversed himself. "No, wrong. Autobiographical first, then Israel. Change of pace." As simply as that the decision was taken, and I next wrote the novel closest to my heart, a kaddish for my father, at once the funniest and the saddest of my works, *Inside, Outside.*

PART TWO

THE FIDDLER

CHAPTER FIVE

Inside, Outside

Last Hurrah of the Funnyman

WHY IS *INSIDE, OUTSIDE* the novel closest to my heart? Well, to begin with the book is *funny*, often laugh-out-loud funny. Molière called comedy "the strange métier of making honest folks laugh"; and that was my métier, until the war years turned me into something of a heavy dog. So I can briefly turn serious in passages about the life and death of my father, and sentimental or, if you will, schmaltzy, about my childhood and family in the Jewish Bronx of the 1920s.

On the first page of *Inside, Outside* I take the artistic license of a memoir novel to show up in the persona of one I. David Goodkind, a Wall Street tax

lawyer, in his youth a radio gagman, who has been appointed a "cultural assistant" in the Nixon White House, mainly to write jokes for his speeches. Goodkind and his wife are lifelong Democrats. Her reaction, as the book tells it: *"She inquired how I would like a divorce . . . but the man holds our present destiny in his hands, does he not? He worked his way into that position despite . . . the political record of a polecat. To observe him might be broadening . . ."* And like a true son of my father, Goodkind adds, *"Placed here I might somehow, at some moment, do something for our Jewish people. The Talmud says, 'A man can earn the world to come in a single hour.' "*

That last sentence drives the novel.

Writing in his book-lined White House office, with Watergate raging outside and little to do, Goodkind resumes an abandoned memoir of his life (mine, that is), backing up to the departure of my mother from Minsk for America at sixteen, followed by my father's emigration, also from Minsk to the Golden Land. They meet in New York and marry, and I am born after my sister Lee, though I am clearly the family jewel, the circumcised one. The novel rambles through the comedy of my childhood years, teen years, college years, and early loves, up to and through my gagman days. Much of the amusement arises from the relatives

my father brings over from the old country: first his mother, "Bobbeh," my grandma, whose arrival in our fifth-floor back Bronx flat puts my mother's nose out of joint. A crisis that erupts over Bobbeh's sauerkraut crocks may be the funniest sequence I have ever written; and Bobbeh's encounter with Mr. Winston, my dandyish English teacher who wears spats, and comes to recruit me for boys' camp, still makes me laugh when I reread it.

Of my bar mitzvah Goodkind gives a true picture, downright comical yet at key moments solemn. This is the note he strikes about all our religious observances, including the holidays and the way they clash with college schedules and fraternity life. Such comic scenes about growing up give place to another vein of humor entirely, once Peter Quat and I become joke writers for Harry Goldhandler. The slapstick farce of the Gag Czar's antics, juggling weekly programs for several comedians at the same time, is a comedy of pain, the pain of a gifted writer scrambling for enough money to live with his family in a Central Park West penthouse, until he dies overnight.

The serio-comic memoir is halted briefly by an alarm in Washington over Arab army movements on Israel's borders. This calms down and Goodkind with it. Goodkind has been a Zionist of sorts, like most

American Jews, only since Israel's lightning victory in the Six-Day War of 1967. My father was a lifelong Zionist, but as Goodkind writes, during my growing up I was bored by all that Palestine stuff, even joking about it in a humor column in my college newspaper. My first glimpse of Israel was in fact casual. When *Marjorie Morningstar* came out in 1955, a newly formed America-Israel Society invited me and my wife, all expenses paid, to join a delegation bringing a replica of the Liberty Bell to celebrate Israel's seventh year of independence.* We decided, "Why not?"

Israel then had a million and half Jews, a third of them driven from Arab lands. It was an exciting, raw, not comfortable place, but our welcome was heartwarming. Sarah and I were feted. *The Caine Mutiny Court-Martial* in Hebrew was put on for us in the Habima Theater. Prime Minister David Ben-Gurion met us during an intermission and invited us to his kibbutz in the Negev, where he urged us to come and live in Israel. In *This Is My God,* I write a lot about that conversation with Ben-Gurion. The chapter concludes, "The little land by a far stretch may some day support four million Jews." Israel at last count has about seven million Jews, a world leader in high tech, a formidable

---

* The bell hangs today in a Jerusalem park.

embattled military force. How far off the mark could I get? Such, however, was the first honest misimpression of an almost prototypical American Jew.

———

As my clear-eyed wife points out on page four of this book, I am "not that interesting a person." So Goodkind (good *kind*) concentrates on the merriment, innocent or painful, of my early life. Beyond those years he takes considerable artistic liberties. He gives me a feisty daughter I never had, and expands on a romance my sister Lee did have in a visit to Palestine after college, ages ago. As a gray-haired country-club widow, my real-life sister was roundly ragged about this passage by her grown-up sons and her club friends. Both inventions tied the story much closer to Israel, and if, as my sister told me, her part was written in her heart's blood, well, that's a writer for you.

The imaginary daughter, Sandra, is a college-campus rebel of the Vietnam years, fiercely anti-Israel and working on a thesis, *The Israeli Peace Movement: Progressive Counter-currents in a Proto-Fascist State.* Also, she has a thing going with a young American lawyer, Abe Herz, who has made aliya: a powerful physical attraction but a wearing mental mismatch.

During a fresh alarm about Arab troop maneuvers, Goodkind takes leave of the President and flies to Israel because his aged infirm mother has been hospitalized there; and the President gives him a secret verbal message for Golda Meir. Sandra invites herself along on his flight, goes to a radical kibbutz for research on her thesis, and from there she writes a letter to her parents, a searching, bristly analysis of where she is at in life, a pivot of all the book's themes.

Back at his job once his mother improves, Goodkind finds a vastly different emergency engulfing the White House. A minor witness at the Senate committee probe of Watergate has mentioned that tapes were secretly recorded in the President's office. National shock! Nothing now interests the President but urgent damage control. He receives Golda Meir's verbal reply with an absent nod and an offhand dismissal, and Goodkind realizes he has become superfluous; but reluctant to leave the President in the lurch, he holes up in his office and scrawls at his memoir while troubles rain down on Nixon's head. The Senate subpoenas the tapes. He rejects the subpoenas. The vice president is unmasked as a crook, but fights resigning. At a serious full mobilization of the armed forces of Egypt and Syria on Israel's borders, the U.S. secretary of state warns Israel not to preempt with an air strike.

On Yom Kippur, when all activity ceases in Israel for a day of prayer, thousands of tanks roll in north and south and achieve total military surprise.

Just then, notified that his mother has had a relapse and may be dying, Goodkind hastens without a by-your-leave to her on an El Al plane jammed with Israelis returning to serve in the war. He finds her in an oxygen tent, barely conscious. "So you're here?" she gasps, feebly clasping his hand. "Go and fight." On the radio in his Jerusalem hotel suite, as he tries to phone Sandra on the kibbutz's one telephone line, he hears General "Dado" Elazar, the army Chief of Staff, claim at a press conference that the war has turned around, and "we are now breaking their bones." The kibbutz reports that Sandra is gone, nobody knows where. Goodkind is startled by a call from the hotel switchboard, "Hold for the Prime Minister's office."

"Doovidel." Golda Meir's unmistakable rough voice. He has known her for years, ever since he did tax work on Israel bonds. "How is your mother?" Not at all surprised by her inquiry in the midst of war— this is Israel, after all—he gives her the doctors' cheering report. "Good you came, Doovidel. Still, you might help us by going back tonight."

When he arrives in Washington, a U.S. Air Force helicopter whirls him through a drizzle to Camp

David. He delivers a handwritten letter from the Prime Minister to Nixon, sitting shirtsleeved by a fire. The President reads it carefully twice, sunk in an armchair, then drops it into the fire. He chats for a while, not much to the point, then rouses himself and dismisses Goodkind. The novel goes on, with Goodkind thinking in despair:

> *Yet in Israel, everything depended now on the word of this one distracted, dejected, hounded, played-out, incredibly hated man in shirt sleeves, the President of the United States.*
>
> *"Sir," I blurted, "may I say one thing before I go?"*
> *He barely nodded.*
> *"Mr. President, the people with the longest historical memory in the world are the Jews. The Israelis can hold off the Arabs, though they're out-numbered in manpower. They can match them and beat them. The one thing they can't match is the airlift that's bringing their enemies the output of the Soviet Union's munition plants. They're only three million people."*
> *"I'm aware of that," the President said in a dry tone.*
> *"Sir, I don't know the latest intelligence, but I know how I felt when I saw Golda Meir's face.*

If you order an airlift now to match the Soviet shipments—<u>now</u>, sir—then the world's longest historical memory will honor you forever." In those remote, infinitely tired eyes, I thought I saw a dusky glimmer. I plunged ahead. "It will honor the man who showed greatness, by rising above his own desperate political predicament and coming to the rescue of the Jewish State."

The President said nothing for a while, staring at the dying fire, then he tiredly pushed himself up out of his armchair. "Well, I may have to kick some ass, at that. The thing has been batting back and forth all week between State and Defense."

He walked with me to the door and shook hands. "You've stayed aboard while some others were jumping ship. It's been appreciated."

Such is I. David Goodkind's Talmudic "single hour": a decidedly nervy exercise, I daresay, of literary license. Here *Inside, Outside* really ends. We last glimpse Goodkind on an El Al flight from Israel after the war, returning from what he terms "this bizarre Technicolor interlude" in his career to the drab black and white of tax law. The various subplots of his early life have been wound up, his mother is better, Sandra

is staying with her wounded soldier, Abe Herz, and the taxman is writing the last words of his memoir.

What really happened in this war, after all? Would a preemptive strike have stopped the Arabs in their tracks? Would it have alienated the Americans? The Arabs alienated nobody by striking first, that's self-evident. Over all looms the question that more and more haunts me: how did a people that thirty years ago marched docilely into gas chambers by the millions, women, children, and all, turn around in a generation to become one of the most impressive armed forces on earth? There is the military miracle that I don't begin to fathom. Who does? Where are the books? What is the answer? If I can't find a book that tells me in plain English what I want to know, maybe I'll dig for the truth and write one myself . . .

Which eventually I did in *The Hope* and *The Glory,* though, as with the Main Task, one war novel became two.

———

The reception of *Inside, Outside* surprised me. It became a number one bestseller and earned the warmest critical press of any of my books. On the front page of *The New York Times Book Review,* James Michener paid rare homage to *Inside, Outside.* The literary light of my day, Joe Heller, author of *Catch-22,* sent me an eloquent letter of praise and gratitude for writing the book.* All in all, a wonderful result for a self-indulgent memorial novel, a chancy labor of love.

---

* See Note.

CHAPTER SIX

The Hope and *The Glory*

RECENTLY I READ A story in an Israeli newspaper on the Internet, about seven IDF warplanes landing at sea on a nuclear aircraft carrier, the U.S.S. *Theodore Roosevelt*. The photos showed some carrier officers greeting the Jewish airmen on the flight deck, IDF fighter jets taking off and landing, and aircraft in a re-fueling exercise; and I was struck, all of a heap, by the amazing changes in the fortunes of my Jewish people during the hundred years of my life.

Menachim Begin, the Israeli Prime Minister who negotiated the historic peace treaty with Egypt's President Anwar Sadat, once told me that he planned to

write an ambitious history, *The Jewish People: Destruction and Resurgence,* after he retired from politics. Begin was an able, unashamedly partisan historian, and he might well have done such a book, for—rather like Winston Churchill—he was a leading figure in the history he wrote about. Unlike Churchill, alas, Begin was worn out by his travails in office and died early. He lives on in world history, sharing the Nobel Peace Prize with Anwar Sadat. A grandiose literary concept like Menachim Begin's has never been mine; yet, looking back over my works, I can trace a shadowy American version of his theme, complete to a Resurgence novel that became two long novels.

———

Faithful reader, allow a cheerful centenarian to drop back many years, very briefly. When Israel declared independence in 1948, I had two short comic novels to my name. My third book, *The Caine Mutiny,* gave that name a sound, *Marjorie Morningstar* a louder sound. In fact, *Marjorie* earned Sarah and me our first trip to Israel. After that first visit,* we came to Israel often. My Hebrew speaking improved. Israelis

---

* See *This Is My God,* Little, Brown and Company, 1959, Chapter 22.

stopped saying with a smile that I sounded like a Bible character. An Israel novel? For a certainty, I would one day write such a book! My very first notion was to create an Israeli Tevye, and as Shalom Aleichem brought to life the vanished Jewry of Eastern Europe with his Tevye, so I would with my Tevye bring to life the new Jewish state. Novelists have such brainstorms, an occupational hazard. The more I learned about Israel, the less I felt up to being its Shalom Aleichem; not to mention that this Jewry, far from vanishing, was making a prodigious comeback.

On leaving New York for good in late 1959, Sarah and I discussed spending time in Israel to improve our boys' Hebrew, but the Main Task was urgently on my mind, requiring years of intense research not feasible in Israel. We brought to St. Thomas in the Caribbean a trunkful of World War II books and volumes on military history. For six long years, I moiled through that trunkful, becoming a pro tem military historian while scrawling at *Youngblood Hawke,* and for relief, at my island frolic, *Don't Stop the Carnival.* Back in the U.S.A., we settled in Washington where I started actual writing of the Main Task, and it was there that I became friendly with the Israeli ambassador, the keen mild-mannered Avram Harman. One morning before services at the Georgetown synagogue, the

rabbi showed up saying, "Agnon is here." AGNON!!
As soon as I got home I phoned Abe Harman. Yes,
S. Y. Agnon would indeed address a thousand Con-
servative rabbis that day at a banquet lunch, and as
chairman he would put us at a front table.

I had never seen Agnon or a photo of him. The
first Hebrew author to win a Nobel Prize was a little
man in a big black yarmulke, who read a speech entirely in Hebrew with the pages to his face. When he
finished and sat down, the thousand American rabbis
politely applauded. Ambassador Harman thereupon
jumped up, a man transformed. This was late in May
1967, when Egypt's President Nasser had closed the
Strait of Tiran, and it looked like war. "We do not want
one inch of another nation's soil," thundered Harman,
shaking clenched raised fists, "but if we're attacked,
we'll fight and *win!*" That brought on a standing ova-
tion. A ministry person asked Sarah and me quietly:
could we possibly host Agnon for dinner? The ambassador was beset by events, and Agnon was strictly kosher. Sarah at once agreed. The Israeli military attaché
in mufti, and the fund-raisers who had Agnon in tow,
brought him to our house. That is how I came to know
Josef Geva, a main consultant on my Israel Novels.
During that dinner, Geva kept discreetly slipping out
and back in, no doubt tracking the war news, as Agnon

wolfed down helpings of Sarah's quiche, while telling me about the Nobel banquet, where he was served on gold plates. The King of Sweden, sitting beside him, assured him they had been kashered. "I thanked him," said Agnon puckishly, "and I didn't eat."

After dinner I took him back to his hotel suite, and we talked far into the night. He was appalled at the expense of his lavish suite. "Look at this," he said, gesturing around, "and I'm a poor man." He had read none of my work, he did not read English; but a lady neighbor had given away three copies of *The Caine Mutiny,* and evidently between that fact and Sarah's quiche, the great man was taken with me. Whenever I came to Israel after that, we would meet and talk. Under his religious persona, Shmuel Yosef Agnon was a formidable Berlin intellectual, sharply au courant. Once he even quizzed me at length about James Joyce, though we both gave up that struggle.

———

The Six-Day War of June 1967 remains a wonder of modern military history. In *The Hope* I do it up brown, as it were. On June 6, as the Israelis quaked at Nasser's threats and the world's passivity, IDF warplanes wiped out all neighboring Arab air forces on

the ground in a few morning hours. The ground troops then advanced to the Suez Canal and clear down the whole Sinai Peninsula, while in the north they took all Jerusalem and captured the Golan Heights.

Sarah and I came with the boys to Israel late in July. The stunning victory was everywhere manifest—the airport thronged with foreigners (mostly Americans), brighter bigger new poster ads for hotels, restaurants, tours, car rentals, and limo services. Our hired limo sped up the winding mountain road to Jerusalem; no need now for the crooked Latrun bypass, the IDF held the fortress. From our King David suite we could see the slant road up to the Old City, once deserted and unused, now streaming both ways with buses and cars. A young waiter rolled in our lunch, singing "Jerusalem the Golden" with a proud smile.

I called the number of Josef Geva's army office. "Oh, so you're here? Good! Welcome! Can I do something for you?"

"Do you know Agnon's address?"

"I'll drive you there."

In uniform, Geva was quite as friendly as he had been in mufti. Outside the great author's home, signs in Hebrew cautioned SILENCE! Agnon himself, surprised and delighted to see me, thanked Geva and

took charge, donning a worn fedora to bring me to a large gathering on folding chairs in the sun, where a speaker was flamboyantly asserting that Israel must keep all the regained territories and not yield one inch. Agnon applauded happily, just another old Israeli in an old hat; Arab rioters had once destroyed his Jerusalem house, with all his Berlin records and manuscripts. The rally organizers pressed me to speak, but I sensed that identifying the *Caine Mutiny* author as one of them was a dumb idea. Back at his home, Agnon showed me his workroom. A stand-up desk was piled with letters; "I haven't answered any," he said plaintively. A beautiful old lady looked in and answered a question he asked her with two words, *"Pahot k'dye"* ("Not enough"), and withdrew. Gossip was rife about Agnon, so I had heard that when he turned back to the religion, his wife had not.

Geva returned me to the King David. About the rally, he seemed if anything sadly amused. "We'll have lunch with Lova Eliav after you've toured a bit," he said. "I introduced my old friend to you in Washington." I didn't remember Lova Eliav but let it pass.

———

My wife and the boys loved the sightseeing, if not quite as I did. From my upbringing in Hebrew schools of the old Bronx, these were magic names and scenes, blocked to view before the war by walls of sandbags in Jerusalem, fenced off elsewhere with heavy barbed wire. Now we could stroll from the King David down to the Western Wall (no longer the Wailing Wall!). We drove down to Jericho and up to Mount Gerizim, where the Samaritans showed us their quite different Torah. We did Israel, in short, from Sharm el Sheikh in the south to the source of the Jordan River in the north, most moved (at least I was) by the cave in Hebron where our fathers Abraham, Isaac, and Jacob are interred with Sarah, Rebecca, and Leah, all but Rachel, whose tomb we also saw. This was the LAND after all, I thought. The hardliners might be making pretty good sense, at that.

So I said to Josef Geva, not much to his surprise, when he came to take me to lunch with "Lova" Eliav. At the noted Shemesh (Sun) restaurant we met Lova, and then I did remember him: a small man with a fabled background as a blockade runner. Evading the destroyers of the British Mandate, Lova Eliav had brought many shiploads of refugees from Nazi-ruined Europe to the Holy Land. He was a gentle quiet sort,

not a trace of Rhett Butler about him. "So, you tend to agree with Agnon about the territories?" he asked.

"Well, sort of, but then, I really don't know anything."

"Not true, you're a well-informed American Jew. Too many Israelis are thinking the same way."

Lova talked about his own political background. For a while he had been Golda Meir's executive secretary, closer to her than anyone else. His sympathy for the Palestinians had been his undoing. "She cut me off at the knees," he said without rancor. "I haven't changed my mind. We can't hold down two million slaves forever." That one remark from our Shemesh lunch I remember word for word. In the years that followed Lova would visit me in Washington, usually after a war, when he would swiftly draw a diagram of Israel's new borders, explaining his vision of how they should be maintained or changed. He held a respected place in Israeli public opinion as their one utterly honest man, the irreproachable peacenik, and to some an amiable cuckoo.

I came back from Israel all charged up with Zionism. Exciting notions for "the Israel Novel" flitted through my mind on the flight home and faded as the El Al plane touched down in Dulles. My mother,

who flew there every summer while my grandfather was alive, was wont to say, "Israel is an inspiration, but it fades." Hardheaded Mama, bless her memory. My sons call our return to Washington the *Braina der Kechen* time: I was still reading Shalom Aleichem to them on Friday night, though the elder was soon off to Princeton. In "Rabchik," the story of a homeless always famished dog, Rabchik gets caught in a kitchen door slammed on him by a mean old cook (*kechen*) named Braina. The real-life Braina was an old kosher cook who fed all of us, in a three-room apartment across the street from "the purple house"—the N Street House, as we now called it—while Sarah was restoring the run-down 1815 Federal town house to its pristine style. Washington cliff dwellers all know that N Street is a premier Georgetown address. We were insiders right off, such as we had never been on Park Avenue in soulless Manhattan. The little old synagogue at one end of N Street was our kind of shul.

The Winds of War became quite a success, though the story was only half told. While I took on writing the sequel, the Israel Novel perforce went on a back burner. The Holocaust loomed as a black horror utterly beyond my powers, but I had to attempt it. First, however, Sarah and I agreed that I needed a break.

———

Some years earlier, in a London synagogue, an affluent South African gentleman had invited me to lecture in Cape Town. Half kidding, I had said I would do it for a kosher safari. Now, years later, he cabled me. The kosher safari was on; interested? Sarah and I did not hesitate long. Chance of a lifetime, perfect moment between two huge writing tasks. We go! Washington to London, thence to South Africa, such was the long way there. Forewarned by travel books, Sarah, like other ladies in the crowded first class, brought along nightdress and robe. She curled up on two empty seats that I had obtained with devious maneuvering I can't recall, but I never forgot her few sleepy words as she dozed off, *"You can do anything, can't you?"* This wife of mine parted with a compliment as she would with her wedding ring, almost. In *War and Remembrance,* those words are my heroine's last speech, addressed to her Navy husband. She has barely survived Auschwitz, and he brings back to her their lost boy.

———

The Kalahari Desert was a vision of Eden out of Genesis. Beasts I had seen since childhood only caged,

or forlorn in fake small habitats—zebras, elephants, giraffes with baby giraffes—grazed there free as air to the horizon, scattered or in herds, under God's deep clear blue sky. The squat tourist lodge marred the vision just a bit. The kosher food proved no problem: all tourist food was flown out from Cape Town anyway. The host lady, showing us into a tented hut, warned us about "Alroy," who might rub up against it. So he did, and the place shook. Alroy was an elephant, colossal at close range, who came and went on the lodge grounds as he pleased; the lady could also shoo him out in exasperation, as she did now for us, and he lumbered off. Young guides in jeeps took us to the watering holes, ringed with wild creatures peaceably crowding each other to drink. Once we emerged from a clump of shrub trees and came upon a moving herd of elephants that stopped, heavily turned, and raised their trunks at us in evident menace. The guide barely muttered, "Don't talk, just whisper," a needless caution to us with our hearts in our mouths. Alas, we did not see lions in the wild; otherwise, all in all, this was about the best thing Sarah and I ever did together, except maybe get married and have the boys. Remember, though, that when I lectured more than forty years ago in Cape Town and Johannesburg, this was apartheid South Africa. Another story. Not Eden.

Back in the U.S.A., wonderfully refreshed by Alroy and his fellow free beasts, and by the fleeting vision of man's lost paradise, I sailed with gusto into writing the new book. The year 1972 melted away, 1973 was speeding by like telephone poles past an express train, and here came another travel time, the High Holy Days and Sukkot. Sarah had devised in our small N Street garden a passable sukkah, but we had taken to going to Israel for those three weeks. This year we elected to try a much praised hotel in Lucerne. Sure enough, it had a beautiful spacious sukkah for Europe's Orthodox Jews. The Yom Kippur War broke out when we were at services in the hotel before Sukkot. The cantor was a tall burly guest from Antwerp, an Auschwitz survivor with a splendid voice, now a well-to-do gentleman in the diamond business, who loved to spread his cantorial feathers during the high holidays. In Lucerne I barely got to talk with the man; the war news was too puzzling and distracting. The following year I traveled after Sukkot to Antwerp just to meet with him.

This was UDAM,* in my Auschwitz chapters the resourceful fellow who befriends my heroine. He got on with the SS by performing obscene ditties or

---

* In one Yiddish dialect, *Adam*.

weepy ballads in their bar, and he could pass in the camp comforting fellow inmates with nostalgic Yiddish songs and cantorial solos. While he talked, there in Antwerp, I felt (as it were) back in that ghastly secret railroad terminal in Poland. I had delved at Yad Vashem into the horrors of Auschwitz. I had read many books by or about survivors and talked with several. This was different, the miasmic place itself in broad daylight; I don't know how else to put it. He was passing on to me, face-to-face, his fine voice hoarsened with emotion, the truth he knew. I have no record of his name. I don't know that he retained mine. We never corresponded after that one meeting in Antwerp. Writing *War and Remembrance,* I had to deal with Auschwitz. UDAM, a chance encounter, helped me create what reality I managed to achieve.

Today when I think back on our research travels, not Auschwitz but Tehran comes first to mind. There Roosevelt, Churchill, and Stalin forged the ring that closed on the fiercely resisting German nation, and rid the planet and them of the maniac who led them to commit their unprecedented crimes. We saw the embassies and talked to some Russians. Churchill in his history gives a biting account of his birthday banquet at the British Embassy, where Stalin asked to give the last toast. He rose and made it, not to the birthday boy

but to Lend-Lease, obliquely to Roosevelt, "without which we would lose the war." Stalin's crude gesture then and there epitomized the shift in world power.

———

Main Task II was in the bookstores. The Israel Novel was next, until, as the reader may recall, my editor calmly reversed himself with "No, no, that's expected of you, but autobiographical novel first, change of pace." Whether by luck or foresight, Ned Bradford made the crucial decision of my latter years. Had I then begun the Israel Novel, Autobiographical might well have faded off unwritten. This way I went to work on it, and we rented a small Jerusalem apartment where we could come and go, while I dug into military documents in Hebrew, read memoirs, and boned up on Israeli history, especially of the Yom Kippur War. We had then been in Lucerne, anxiously reading foreign newspapers, listening to foreign broadcasts, trying to follow what was happening, during all that three-week life-or-death ordeal of the Jewish state. I retained only a hazy idea of the actual events. Now I could talk to politicians and army leaders, some retired, some still hot in the action, a few who spoke only Hebrew. None of this, however, was yet coming to life.

Among the pictures on my workroom walls, mostly family, the largest is a cover of *Life* magazine (now extinct) dated June 23, 1967. The caption was WRAP-UP OF THE ASTOUNDING WAR. AN ISRAELI SOLDIER COOLS OFF IN THE SUEZ CANAL. The smiling youngster is up to his chest in water, brandishing a captured Kalashnikov. I did not actually meet the fellow until many years later. An engaging history by Chaim Herzog, *The War of Atonement,* mentioned one Yossi Ben Hanan, a colonel on his honeymoon in Nepal who left his bride, zigzagged home on any available flights, and arrived on the second day of the war. His father met him with his uniform. He led his tank brigade up the Golan Heights, where a small Israeli tank force was battling the massive surprise onslaught of Syrian tanks, and helped stem the tide. Then, in a daring foray behind enemy lines he was badly wounded, rescued with difficulty, and went on fighting the war.

I tried to track down this bizarre Ben Hanan through the army but was stonewalled—by bureaucracy, or secrecy, or obtuse stupidity, who could say? It occurred to me to call Josef Geva, long since retired from the military, now an industrialist with a plant in Haifa. When I explained, he laughed. "Why didn't you ask me first? He's my cousin." I phoned the Haifa hospital where Ben Hanan was in bed after minor surgery,

reading, as it happened, *The Winds of War*. I told him how I admired what I had learned about him in *The War of Atonement*. "Oh, that's all horseshit," he said. A short chapter in *The Will to Live On** is all about Yossi. In U.S. Navy lingo, he would have been dubbed an "original," that is, an outstanding but off-the-wall senior officer. He became my primary resource for the land warfare in the sands of Sinai, from platoon duty to grand strategy. In time he rose to command the tank corps. Upon retiring as a major general, he represented Israel's military industry abroad for years. Yossi Ben Hanan is today my closest friend who is still alive.

With Yossi as consultant, I could at last tackle the Israel Novel. I got at it with a will, riding a surge of renewed zest for combat narrative. I drove head-down through Israel's early history like a man possessed. The Bible tells us that Jacob's seven years of service for Rachel "went by like a few days, because he so loved her." Something like that was animating me as I wrote and wrote, and *wrote,* and delivered a truly gigantic manuscript to Little, Brown.

A silence ensued. It became long. It became disquieting. One morning the lady of my life came into my office, plunked herself down on a chair and said

---

* My sequel to *This Is My God.*

brightly, "Well, they don't like it." That is exactly how it went. An inner voice had been grumbling as the years passed, *"Look, this feels like you're writing two books, not one,"* but I had shrugged it off as the mere angst of an aged author (by then approaching eighty!). Now my wife as agent had her hands full between a publisher balking at an enormous sprawling literary work, and a husband-author fulminating with outraged ego. The redoubtable Cy Rembar resolved the brief crisis by reading the thing and remarking to the publishers that they were getting two Herman Wouk war novels for a royalty advance on one. In that insensate drive, I had rough-drafted both *The Hope* AND *The Glory*! Grasping Cy's point, the publishers cheered up mightily, decided they loved the vast artifact, and sent out one William Phillips, a keen New York editor, to work on it with me in Palm Springs.

Bill's take on our job was incisive and strictly business: *hero first!* But that was no simple matter. My four leading characters were all my friends, army men given made-up names. Meir Amit had headed the Mossad; he became *Sam Pasternak*. The Air Force chief was Benny Peled (*Benny Luria*). Josef Geva, the Vienna-born intellectual, a contender for Chief of Staff diverted into diplomacy, I called *Zev Barak*. I had Yossi in mind as hero (*Yossi Nitzan, "Don Kishote"*) for

his risk-taking bravery bordering on the crazy; but it became clear that Bill had it right: Zev Barak was our man, emerging from the excessive verbiage.

My outpouring of this work was altogether peculiar. I barreled along more or less as I pleased, using my friends to act out the real events, which I had arduously researched, while endowing them with fictional wives, children, and lovers. These figments intermingled with the real persons to grow, change, marry, divorce, have affairs, and grow old. You may ask how, at my advanced age, I could possibly have hoped to produce two such large works on such a special theme. Well, first of all, I could not then conceive that it could end up, like the Main Task, as two volumes; second, Ned Bradford had said of the Israel Novel, "it's expected of you." So I plunged in and did my best. Bill Phillips then came along and we carved out the books. Yossi Ben Hanan once remarked to me in passing, "You love this postage stamp of a country, don't you?" Enough said.

———

Bill's best contribution to the work struck me at first as onerous; he wanted me to make the giant script longer still, by including Entebbe and Osirak, two

sensational Air Force missions some years after the Yom Kippur War. My draft manuscript ended with the Begin-Sadat peace. There was no going past it, I thought, marking as it did Israel's transit from the beleaguered "Zionist entity" to a democratic nation in the Middle East. True enough, yet those feats did confirm the Jewish state's presence in current events as a strong player. Entebbe won the world's admiration when four IDF transport planes flew two thousand miles to an airport in Uganda, Central Africa, and rescued the Jewish hostages in a hijacked French airliner; IDF commandos killed the hijackers, who were threatening to murder them, and brought them back to Israel. Osirak incurred almost as much world criticism (but secret relief) by destroying Saddam Hussein's nearly finished nuclear reactor. In my research time, I once talked to the youngest of the four bomber pilots who had dived on Osirak. By then Ilan Ramon was a handsome amiable senior officer with a wife and children. He showed me his tracking book of the flight, and talked freely about flying near Baghdad and back for the split-second diving operation. Ramon later trained in the U.S.A. as an astronaut, and was one of the six who died in the crash of America's shuttle *Columbia*; to this day, the only foreign aviator post-

humously awarded the Congressional Space Medal of Honor.

———

I had told Ned Bradford that I wanted to write two books before I died, one on Israel, one on my life story. By God's grace I have done both, and in this reminiscent glance, I have sketched how I did them.

The Hope begins with an American colonel, David "Mickey" Marcus, who volunteered to serve in Israel's War of Independence, was appointed by Ben-Gurion as "the first Jewish general in two thousand years," and fell in a tragic accident. *The Glory* concludes with Ilan Ramon. This picture of my years in American literature that I fancifully call "The Sailor," with its klezmer soundtrack "The Fiddler," here ends, and I dedicate it to their memories.

Now for a parting word by the cheerful centenarian.

Epilogue

Superfluous lags the veteran on the stage . . .

THIS LINE FROM SAMUEL JOHNSON'S solemn poem "The Vanity of Human Wishes" was haunting me long after *The Glory* came out to lackluster sales and reviews. Quite predictable for a sequel, to be sure; but I had put heart and soul into that book, and the account of land battles on Sinai sands, and the turnaround victory with the Canal crossing, were my special pride. All the same, "*Superfluous . . . superfluous . . .*"

Out of the blue Cy Rembar phoned. One Jimmy Buffett was inquiring about the stage rights to *Don't Stop the Carnival*; I had not heard of the man, and, assuming I was dead, he had approached my lawyer. Not an auspicious start, but Jimmy Buffett came to see me in Palm Springs and in his easy-going fashion blew "superfluous" right out of the water. A chat be-

fore lunch under an old olive tree, and I was agreeing that I might do it, and might even write the libretto. My laconic wife, rather to my surprise, approved as agent. "It might be fun" was all she said. "Superfluous" had never surfaced between us. It did not have to.

The show was all Buffett. He composed the lively Caribbean score, raised the money, and produced it. It did not reach Broadway, after some years of on-and-off revision, while he continued his popular tours and I wrote my next book. On the whole my agent was right, it was fun.

The Will to Live On is a sequel, and for readers deeply interested in Judaism, perhaps more substantial, but a sequel it is, an assignment on my to-do literary list. In good heart, I could go back to writing a novel, though "the impossible novel" I had talked about within my family remained a phantom. *A Hole in Texas* is my foray into science and politics. American scientists during a rare détente had once actually, if briefly, helped the Chinese with their atomic efforts. When I read or heard about this I thought, Well, there's a theme for a lightweight amusement. The "hole in Texas" is a real eighteen-mile tunnel dug for the Superconducting Supercollider, a giant project in high-energy physics, abandoned by Congress in favor of the Space Station. The American physicist, the

Chinese lady scientist with whom he has had an early, serious love affair, the congresswoman who leans on him for advice on science, and his slightly jealous wife are all totally fabricated to make a story. The other big fabrication is the whole premise—namely, that the Chinese had beaten America to the Higgs boson. From *Publishers Weekly* and such advance notices came friendly hurrahs for this figment, and the sales were satisfactory.

Remained now the last to-do challenge, my science and religion meditation (the one that took three years, mentioned in my foreword to this book). My editor had been highly hopeful and patient for more than three years, and his reaction over the phone was a charming relief. He had read the pages pen in hand, had made not one comment or change, and would be proud to publish it as is, even naming the pub date! I hung up before I quite realized that he meant a year later. My works, even nonfiction, had hitherto been rushed to press when finished. This was modified rapture, take it or leave it, but then what to do for a whole empty year? How did I know I would live until then?

And so I bethought me of "the impossible novel," an historical saga about the life of Moses. It remained impossible, of course; Scripture had beat me to it some time ago in the Torah. But in my vein of rowdy

comedy, could I not try what the French, who have precise terms for belles lettres, call a jeu d'esprit or, more exactly, a *sotie*? Was I not, in my high school Latin, in extremis?

There came rolling into my life in a wheelchair, one leg up on a board, Louis Gluck, an Australian uranium billionaire. A very Orthodox old Jew, Gluck is determined to have produced a great accurate movie about Moses—money no object—and he is sure I am the only one who can write it. In the end, what's more, he almost has his way. I perforce become part of the story, Sarah too, in my actual last novel, called *The Lawgiver,* about an imaginary film called *The Lawgiver.* I much enjoyed sending up the movie people in this maze of a tale; and my picture of the devil-dance in Hollywood over such a pot of money is far from wholly fictitious. In changing publishers, I found myself back at Simon & Schuster, publishers of *Aurora Dawn.* Dick Simon is gone, Max Schuster is gone, nobody is there from the old days; but corporations that do well can last indefinitely, unlike centenarians.

Rothschild's Clock Stops

Until recently I kept a frank private diary, which ran to more than a hundred bound volumes. It will remain private. Call it my nature, or a pose, or what you will, the adjective most often attached to my name has been "reclusive." Now it must stand. Rothschild's clock has stopped.

The view from 100 is, to this centenarian, illuminating and surprising. With this book I am free: from contracts, from long-deferred to-do books, in short, from producing any more words. I have said my say, done my work. At thirty, I was retiring from the U.S.S. *Southard,* an old destroyer-minesweeper, to go ashore, claim my bride, and set out for fame and fortune. She was six years younger and irreligious; she took on my Judaism with me. She saw me through most of my hundred years. Our first meeting and our lifelong love are the spine of my longest novel, *Youngblood Hawke,* transmuted by fiction to a nightmare tale of what might have happened to me had we not met and loved. In general, I am rather a head-in-the-clouds fellow; Betty Sarah, beautiful and deep, with an unshakably level head, saw me through the multifarious temptations and traps for a writer in publishing, the-

ater, and films. Her lifelong task done, she left me at ninety. I will join her in God's good time, to rest on the other side of our firstborn son, Abe.

We have had three sons. I have written briefly in this book, never before or since, of our firstborn son, Abe, a radiant memory. Wherever in my works I have written of death, it has been, in one way or another, about Abe. Natalie's threatened son Louis, in *War and Remembrance,* is close to Abe's portrait, but that little boy I allowed to survive. Our youngest son passed the bar in New York and California, then elected to go to Israel and volunteer for the Navy. He lives now in Eilat, and we learn the Talmud each Sunday morning, face-to-face on Skype. The son closest to me here in Palm Springs is a writer with a variegated tale of his own to tell. He once saved several early volumes of my diary that I wanted him to destroy. I hope he will edit my diary, if both sons agree to publish any of it.

In it, for anyone interested, there is the whole Herman Wouk story. How, for instance, when I turned forty, Columbia, my alma mater, put on a public exhibit of my manuscripts, which I thought kind of premature. I wrote a wry article about it, "On Being Under Glass." By fifty I had acquired the knowledge and the maturity to attempt the Main Task, a global panorama of World War II, in which I meant to embed the Holo-

caust. I did not know whether I would live to complete it or whether people would read it if I did. My sixties and seventies went to finding that out. Other things in the literary life may have ceased to matter that much, but I have always loved the work.

NOTE

January 13, 1989

Dear Herman:

About five days ago I did something I should have done a few years ago. I began reading <u>Inside Outside</u>. And from the moment I started I found myself just about unable to stop. My own work slipped into the background. Only when my eyes grew tired was I able to give spare time to anything else, and long before I finished I knew I was going to write you this letter of praise and gratitude. The book is funny, warm, perceptive, engrossing, exciting, titillating, and, for me, exuberantly instructive. It radiates with an affection and tenderness that moves me still to laughter and tears. I know more about Yidishkeit than I ever knew before, more about talmudic studies, more about Israel, and I have a greater respect for the devotional attitudes underlying our Jewish religious observances than I have ever had in my life.

Any thoughts I occasionally entertain of writing an account of my own about growing up in Coney Island during the depression will be put aside for a long, long time. If I did try such a work, I'm afraid I would want to use your relatives instead of mine, especially your Zaideh and your father, and many of your acquaintances and work experiences. As you state, the book is a eulogy to your father, and it probably is the most affecting eulogy to which I have ever been witness.

From the outside, Herman, it appears you have led a richly varied, successful, beneficial, and fulfilling life. I hope sincerely that it has been true for you on the inside too.

In all sincerity,
Joseph Heller

ABOUT THE AUTHOR

HERMAN WOUK is the author of such classics as *The Caine Mutiny* (1951), *Marjorie Morningstar* (1955), *Youngblood Hawke* (1961), *Don't Stop the Carnival* (1965), *The Winds of War* (1971), *War and Remembrance* (1978), and *Inside, Outside* (1985). His later works include *The Hope* (1993), *The Glory* (1994), *A Hole in Texas* (2004), and *The Lawgiver* (2012). Mr. Wouk's achievements include the 1952 Pulitzer Prize for Fiction for *The Caine Mutiny*; appearing on the cover of *Time* magazine for *Marjorie Morningstar,* the bestselling novel of that year; and the cultural phenomenon of *The Winds of War* and *War and Remembrance,* which he wrote over a thirteen-year period and which went on to become two of the most popular novels and TV miniseries events of the 1970s and 1980s. In 2008, Mr. Wouk was honored with the first Library of Congress Lifetime Achievement Award for the Writing of Fiction. He lives in Palm Springs, California.